Wide seas and many lands

Arthur Mason

Nabu Public Domain Reprints:

You are holding a reproduction of an original work published before 1923 that is in the public domain in the United States of America, and possibly other countries. You may freely copy and distribute this work as no entity (individual or corporate) has a copyright on the body of the work. This book may contain prior copyright references, and library stamps (as most of these works were scanned from library copies). These have been scanned and retained as part of the historical artifact.

This book may have occasional imperfections such as missing or blurred pages, poor pictures, errant marks, etc. that were either part of the original artifact, or were introduced by the scanning process. We believe this work is culturally important, and despite the imperfections, have elected to bring it back into print as part of our continuing commitment to the preservation of printed works worldwide. We appreciate your understanding of the imperfections in the preservation process, and hope you enjoy this valuable book.

WIDE SEAS AND MANY LANDS

WIDE SEAS
AND MANY LANDS

By
ARTHUR MASON
With an Introduction by
MAURICE BARING

NEWNES : LONDON

PRINTED IN GREAT BRITAIN

CONTENTS

CHAP.		PAGE
	Preface	7
	Introduction	9
I	An Irish Lad's Beginnings	17
II	Hounded	24
III	Conquests	29
IV	Off to Sea	34
V	My First Voyage	38
VI	Jilted	43
VII	Liverpool Jack	48
VIII	An Escape	55
IX	Bugaboo	60
X	A Courageous Captain	64
XI	The Lime Juicer	74
XII	The Fight off Cape Horn	80
XIII	Hoboes	86
XIV	Benefit of Clergy	95
XV	Hogging It	104
XVI	Jackass Brandy Again	114
XVII	Consequences	121
XVIII	The Carpenter's Clutch	129

CONTENTS

CHAP.		PAGE
XIX	Easy Pickings	138
XX	Steamer Lights	145
XXI	Sails and Sailors	151
XXII	And Captains	159
XXIII	Superstitions	166
XXIV	And Reactions	172
XXV	Salmon Fishing	178
XXVI	The Revival of Lida	182
XXVII	A Day of Reckoning	190
XXVIII	Sale Making	199
XXIX	Farewells	203
XXX	The Old Man of the Violet Rock	208
XXXI	Horse Play	223
XXXII	One Who Sang	229
XXXIII	Old Austen Sees Daylight	233
XXXIV	Ireland Again	240

PREFACE

I HAVE been asked to write my biography. Other people have written of their lives, lives of greater value to the world than mine; though possibly mine too has not been without value in some little ways. Lives have been written so interesting in the telling, that sceptical readers have condemned them as adorned.

My story, I believe, is not lacking in excitement; it shall be told simply, and as swiftly and truly as though the years were crossing the paper, crowding me away from youth and toward the Great Adventure.

There may be glued leaves in the volume of my life, but I shall steam them apart, trying to piece out a pattern that is not so much smudged as the background would lead one to suppose.

There will be in the pattern success and failure; heart-cheer and heart-break, such as are in all our lives; such philosophy too as would result from the thinking my life has invited. That there is love to the very end, and will be, as long as I live, speaks not so well for me (for if ever anyone knows the rough-and-tumble of life, I should know it) as it does for human nature.

PREFACE

Surely I may claim to know people, the good of them and the bad; yet I think loving thoughts and incline to loving deeds, and I do believe that the good in me is uppermost and will remain uppermost to the last.

ARTHUR MASON.

INTRODUCTION

It has been noted and deplored that by some curious irony those who have the most interesting things to tell so often do not know how to tell them, while those who have the art of telling at their fingers'-ends have nothing to say. A French critic once pronounced on some writer what Matthew Arnold called a damning sentence:

"*Il dit tout ce qu'il veut mais malheureusement il n'a rien à dire.*"

On the other hand, how often men, and sometimes even women, with the richest stores of original and interesting material at their disposal, not only when they try to present it, fail to do so, but they give us something else, something different. Their personality seems to change, to put on a disguise, to be anything else than what it really is.

But there are at times exceptions to this general rule. It sometimes happens that the writer who really has something to say, is, by nature (and by grace), a born writer. He finds to his surprise that it is as easy to tell his story as it was to live it.

In my opinion, Mr. Arthur Mason should afford us a remarkable example of such an exception. Perhaps I have hit on the reason of this unconscious

INTRODUCTION

mastery of the art of story-telling in the last sentence. Perhaps the reason that he finds it as easy to write his story as it was to live it—although (being an Irishman he will forgive the Irishism) that was extremely difficult—is that in writing his story he lived it over again.

This is perhaps why men and women are tempted, nay are more than tempted, feel impelled and constrained, to write down the story of what they remember. It is not from a desire of imparting information, it is not because they think themselves or what they saw, felt and experienced, particularly interesting or exceptional. It is because they want to live over again the years and the days that are over, and to recall the sights, sounds and smells that have vanished. It is just this power of living a life twice, and of communicating the lights and shadows, the sights and sounds and smells of a dead life to a new generation, which gives so much glamour and magic to their tales.

There are some books, as a man once said, that are a *positive* pleasure to read.

Pre-eminently among such are those which seem to do the work for you. You are not reading at all; you are sitting in a chair, and someone is telling you a story; and you see, as if you were there present, strange scenes, and take part in extraordinary situations, incur dangers, face risks and overcome obstacles. You make friends, meet with enemies, in many lands, under strange skies, and in alien landscapes. For instance, in this book you run

INTRODUCTION

away to sea and you get to know Liverpool Jack, a sailor, intimately, and when, after he has become the chief friend of your hero (who is telling you the story), he drifts away for the first time, you feel not as if you were reading a story, but as if this had happened to you.

"Jack said good-bye to me as he would to a comparative stranger, and started up the railway track singing in his hearty voice the old-time chantey:

"'In Amsterdam there lived a maid.'"

Years after our hero meets him again, only to lose him at once; he, poor fellow, having "drink taken," being run over by a train (having been heard to say as he left a drinking saloon that as there seemed no one to fight with, he guessed he might as well pull a few trains off the line).

"Poor, poor, lonesome Liverpool Jack," says our hero. And we echo his words as for a dear friend.

In a story-book this would have been arranged differently. A writer of fiction would not have dared to leave Liverpool Jack, with his sudden entrances and his abrupt and final exit, at that.

But we, reading of Liverpool Jack in this book, have the feeling that we are face to face with the touch, the magic touch, of reality, and with the authentic glamour of a real and not an imaginary past. Our own nurse, or, maybe, some stray acquaintance, might have told us such a yarn, full

INTRODUCTION

of inconsequent, unexpected happenings, sudden entrances and abrupt exits. The pleasure we get from books of *true* adventure is different from that which we get from books of invented adventure, great as that is.

We read the works of Jules Verne, of Dumas, of H. G. Wells, with pleasure, with rapture, perhaps, but we read with wonder and admiration, knowing all the while that it isn't true and never could be true; but there are other tales that are told us which we read, and which are not only enthralling in themselves, but are still more enthralling because we know, even without asking our Nanny, that they *are* true.

Such are the stories told us by some of the great Russians, such as Tolstoi and Aksakov, and perhaps the most enjoyable of all such stories are those which deal with the sea and with ships. All sea-stories are enjoyable—just like all port is good (some better)—but very often even the landlubber can tell the subtle difference between those sea-stories which are true and those which are, I will not say false, but second-hand and invented. The landlubber knows if they ring true.

Now, Mr. Mason's autobiography is all about seafaring.

" And the beauty and the mystery of the ships,
And the magic of the sea."

You have only to take at random a few sentences from his book, and you will see what I mean when

INTRODUCTION

I say, not only that the book is about the sea, but that it makes the sea and all that belongs to the sea and ships live for the most dusty, dried-up, stay-at-home, prosaic, city-bound, unadventurous landlubber. This, for instance :

" One evening as we were nearing the eastern edge of the Newfoundland Banks it commenced to blow. The mate ordered the main royals clewed up. The barque carried no fore royal. The breeze was too strong for this light sail. Usually it took two men to furl it, but this evening he shouted to me to shin up, and make it fast alone.

" I did get a gasket around it, but I was unable to pull the sail up on the yard the way it should have been, snugly furled. When I came down on deck again it was growing dark. The mate greeted me with an oath and a kick from his Wellington boots.

" ' Get up there,' he roared, ' and get that sail up on the yard, or I'll break every bone in your body.'

" I have often thought of that kick. It sent me aloft again to be with the stars. That night was the first in my life that I felt really alone with them. The barque below me looked like a helpless bug being borne away by the whim of the sea. The light from the binnacle lamp shone on the figure of the helmsman.

" What an insignificant creature he looked ! The very wheel looked like a spider's web, spun for the moths of frail humanity.

" The mate had made me angry, and I was in no hurry to obey him. As I looked at the stars above me, and the restless sea below, I felt that it was worth more than one kick to be allowed the privilege of being alone with one's self on the main royal of a Blue-nose barque in the fine thrill of such a night as this."

Or this :

" If there is one place in the world for Romance, it is under tropical skies in a sailing ship. There the sailor builds his castles, and echoes from the past mingle with his

INTRODUCTION

thoughts of some pretty girl in a far-away seaport. Sailors get sentimental when the trade winds blow. They are more cleanly in their habits, too, than in the northern and southern latitudes. It is in the night watches, when the moon shines full and balmy winds fan the sails, that they spin their best yarns of shipwrecks, and sweethearts, and hard-shelled mates. They are Neptune's children, as harmless as their boasts, and as flighty as the flying-fish that skim the dark waters."

Here you have the rarest note of romance, which is struck, in my opinion, when romance and reality go hand in hand. It is the true stories that are the most romantic of all stories.

Some have the gift of living them and some have the gift not only of living but of re-living them in the telling of them, and as they tell them of reflecting and re-echoing and evoking as a wizard the very sounds, scenes and scents they have known long ago, in the words that they use and in the accent and cadence of their phrases.

Mr. Mason's work is of this kind.

The magic of the sea seems to have got into the words that he utters. The sea writes for him just as the woods, the hills and the streams write for Wordsworth.

Here is an instance of what I mean.

"It was the summer of 1925, and I was going to sea again. Not as a sailor before the mast this time, nor as a mate, nor a master, but as a passenger. When the Ambrose Channel was cleared, and the old Scotland Lightship bore away on the starboard beam, I felt the motion of the sea of my youth. As the land faded away, and the sky and sea closed in around me, a sadness came over me. Something was wrong, something different from other times.

INTRODUCTION

"It wasn't like being at sea at all. 'In seven days we'll be in Liverpool,' the first officer told me. I recollected the time I crossed this ocean last. Thirty-six days it took, and hellish days they were, every one of them.

"There wasn't a roll out of this ship, the black smoke that belched out of the smoke-stacks seemed unreal, the bulwarks were far away above the floating water. There were no clanks from blocks nor flop of sails, no running to and fro of naked feet, no blue-nosed mate with the double jaw yelling, 'Lay aloft there, damn youse, and overhaul them topsail buntlines.' All that reminded me of the old days were the ship's bells. Their tone was the same, and faithfully to their age-long responsibility, they chimed the pure Time of the Sun."

There is another point which struck me forcibly after reading Mr. Mason's book for the third time. It is this. The adventures are inconsequent. Hairbreadth escapes happen at every moment. He leaves a ship and joins another, he makes friends, he leaves them, and they leave him never to meet again, or to meet for a moment and then to meet no more ; he never stays away from a fight ; he digs in mines ; he drives a team ; he boxes a priest ; he breeds hogs that die of cholera ; he shoots Mexican bandits ; he meets the strange hermit on the violet Rock, and without malice kills the rattlesnake that for years had guarded the secret cave of the man, which he has made into a shrine for the skeleton of his dead love. But in all this seemingly purposeless chain of events and chaos of seemingly meaningless adventure, you seem to hear snatches of the march and music of a definite rhythm, and you guess at the shape and pattern of some unexplained but clear design, some hidden purpose, and meaning, and

INTRODUCTION

plan, which recall to you the words said in Galilee to the multitude:

"Are not five sparrows sold for two farthings, and not one of them is forgotten before God? but even the very hairs of your head are all numbered."

MAURICE BARING.

CHAPTER ONE

AN IRISH LAD'S BEGINNINGS

ONE often wonders whether the desire to wander is not something more than the fidgeting of a restless soul. I shall not even try to analyse this thing—better leave it to the mystics who are sure of their occult settings, and to the theorists who have never smelled the salt. I would rather trust to the something within me which says that to halt is to decay.

Although my hair is greying and my stride shortening, the spirit of adventure is as fresh in me as on the day I capsized a sail-boat in a squall, and the doctor was called to give aid to my mother. She had fainted at the sight of me sitting on the bottom of the overturned boat. When I was finally rescued my father whipped me, the schoolmaster whipped me, and the good padre gave much wise counsel to a bitter little boy. I was then, in the year 1886, ten years old, and that is nearly forty years ago.

That day was a never-to-be-forgotten one. Then, for the first time, I experienced the joys of isolation and the dangers that make for romantic adventure. The sea and I have been friends;

we have understood each other. The sullen moods, the tranquil, the boisterous, each are blended together in harmony, and he who would love the sea must take her in all her moods. I love the sea, and shall continue to, as long as I have eyes to see the indigo and emerald colouring, and ears to hear the rumbling echoes on crest and crag.

My life, until I was eighteen years old, was spent on the good-sized farm of my father, on the shores of Strangford Lough, in the north-eastern part of Ireland. The last of the eighteen years were happy for me, but sad enough for family and friends. I was wild as a buck on the hills. My mother was constantly praying for me, while my father laid heavy the lash.

There was another to be reckoned with—the village schoolmaster. Short and stubby he was, with a black beard and a pug nose, and eyes that were always searching for the bad that might be in a boy. I branded him one time over his heathery eyebrows with a glass ink-bottle. He's dead now, and I suppose I've forgiven him for the welts he made on my young hide.

There were four in our family, two boys and two girls. My brother was older than I by two years. He was a quiet and unassuming boy, always with his head deep in some book. He was never wild. When the hounds and huntsmen went scurrying after a fox or a deer, he would be satisfied to stay with his books, while I would jump through the schoolroom window and run all day with the horses and dogs.

Yet there were times when I too would be buried deep in a book. History gave me a real thrill. *Pickwick Papers* I never grew weary of reading, and *Bleak House* with its court of chancery haunted me. Out of hell there's no redemption; that much I was supposed to know then, but to me the courts of chancery seemed even worse.

The family, I thought, loved my brother far better than they did me. They were always holding him up to me as a model of behaviour, and surely he was to be admired, for he took adventure like a gentleman, as he did everything. He was a midshipman in Her Majesty's Navy when I was a wilding on the high seas. He died, while still in his youth, in South America, and his death has ever remained a grief to me, for I loved him quite as much as the others did.

What I regret most, as I look back over those early years, is the worry I caused my mother. If it had not been for my wildness her hair would have been black as an eclipsed thundercloud for many of her last years. She was the one, when I had been out hunting ducks in the bogs all night, who would open the door at three or four o'clock in the morning, whispering softly: "Don't wake your father. He thinks that you went to bed early." That was the mother who stayed by me then, as her memory ever has: kind, loving, and long-suffering. The principles of forbearance which she taught me are inadequate when one has to tackle, as I did, a world of selfish and intolerant people, who laugh when you laugh, and yawn when the bumper is empty, while they long for another day when the sea may break a prize more worthy. Nevertheless those principles have stayed in my heart from her example, and I do not think that I am unkind, unloving, or impatient, beyond the dictates of my Celtic nature and the training of the sea.

Mother did not know that a world existed outside the County Down. She has been dead now these many years, and I wonder if her soul's imagination has not, from its infinite view-point, seen the world somewhat as I see it.

Our home overlooked the sea, and within easy view ships passed on their way to lands beyond the horizon. To a boy of ten with a romantic imagination, those strange visitors with white sails and dark hulls spoke an undeniable message as they glided by into haze and adventure. One day I made up a little song that went something like this:

I saw from the beach when the morning was shining,
A barque o'er the waters move gloriously on.

Come, youth, it seemed to say, come along with me, over the seas we'll go. Don't whine there, with the dust of the evening hazing your eyes. Up with you, and away to the lands where the natives whitewash their hair, and the yams grow the size of wash-tubs. Rouse yourself! Can't you see the green of the cocoanut groves? Left on the beach, I gazed with desire into a nothingness of lonesomeness. I had to wait the passing of slowly rolling years before I could respond to that call, but those years brought me a good that I did not appreciate then — a well-nourished, strongly proportioned frame, fit for fighting and endurance, an eye more than usually steady, and an unusual knowledge of that most difficult seamanship—navigation of small boats along a rocky coast.

My memories of the old home seem but as those of yesterday, fleeting like scud across my story, leaving pictures of startling brightness here and there: a loving little boy combing his mother's hair and making tea for her when she was sick; land glimpses often—horses and cows and hogs, flax and grist mills, hawthorn hedges in bloom, wild ducks in mating time. Then the wheatfield, when the wheat was in flower and the hawthorn blossoms open to the bumble-bee, and the thrush and meadowlark alternated their song.

I had at an early age a keen curiosity to know all forms of life, and I have studied the habits and customs of wild animals, from rats to sharks. In after years, when the sea claimed me, I once took a sensitive plant with me as a pet on a long voyage. In the early days bird-nest hunting was a favourite pastime. How careful I was when I climbed a tree or a cliff to peer into their nests!

Their eggs must not be disturbed, but it was hard for a boy to keep his hands off them, and I never did. I had to count the eggs and look at their colour, and wonder why some were blue, while others took the colour of pebbles and withered grass. I was told that there was danger of a bird forsaking her nest if she came to know that the hand of man had touched her eggs. There was a way to get around this that would fool the mother-bird. To take the curse off the eggs, you must blow three times on your hands. I always did this, and I never found a forsaken nest.

I must not forget my two dogs, whose instincts were super-animal: who shared my joys and sorrows and were whipped when I was whipped, dragging in with me late at night after I had worn out their poor little legs, trailing me through the bogs hour after hour without food. Then there was Paddy, the Irish hunter, whose soft, nimble lips could fumble any gate until it opened, and whose horse-conscience allowed much gleaning in forbidden pastures in defiance of human stupidity. Paddy died from old age and not from lack of care. My father may not have had all the fatherly instincts, but his animals were royally cared for, and woe betide the groom who neglected the many variations of their diet or failed to give them a light, clean bed of proper depth!

While I remained at home my father's main worry was to keep me out of sailing boats. In this he was never successful. He was afraid of

AN IRISH LAD'S BEGINNINGS

the sea, and had a horror that he would be drowned some day while trying to rescue me. He is at rest now, in the little crowded graveyard beside those of his own and the many who played together, when he and they were boys.

CHAPTER TWO

HOUNDED

I WAS fourteen when I cut the schoolmaster over the eye. There was a hunt on. The red-coated huntsmen came in swarms, the beagle hounds yelped viciously as they passed the country school. The schoolmaster must have known of the hunt in advance. The windows were down and locked with a trigger catch. The front door also was locked.

The back door opened into a yard that had a high wall around it, and the iron gate that gave on the country road was hasped fast with an iron padlock. To get in or out of the school with such conditions required a quick mind and something more—a ladder. I had the agility of mind all right, and, providentially enough, a step-ladder leaned against the wall to the right of a large blackboard.

A flurry of suppressed excitement, such as schoolrooms only know, buzzed around. The master knitted his brows as he gazed out of the window and down the road, taking in the smartly clad ladies who came loping along bent on the hunt. The clatter of their horses' hoofs rang a clarion-call for me. I raised my hand.

HOUNDED

"Please, sir, may I go out?"

Turning a glowering look on me, he said, in his most arrogant brogue: "There'll be no leave till the hunt goes by."

The better-disciplined boys looked at me, smirking: "Now will you be good," they would have said if they had dared.

I have often thought, in my reading of various mystical cults, that sometime in the back ages I may have been a dog. The dog instinct was certainly strong in me that day. When the hunting-horn sounded I was as instantly responsive as the swiftest beagle that led the hounds. I jumped for the step-ladder and rushed for the back door. In my haste I knocked down a couple of the boys. There was a general uproar, while I, heedless of everything and the consequences, slammed the ladder against the back wall, mounted the steps and emerged into freedom.

The village school was soon left behind me in the distance. I ran through stubble fields and thorn hedges, over pillared gates and stepping stiles. I overtook the hunt, passed the stubby, gouty riders, and knowing the cut-offs, was soon in the midst of the baying beagles. I ran with them till the sun went down.

The stag that provided the chase took to the ocean for safety. He was later rescued by boatmen, only to lead the hunt another day. Weary and empty, I turned homeward with the disappointed hounds: they to be caressed and fed,

I to be beaten and humiliated. My visions of what awaited me from an angry father that night and from an angry schoolmaster the next day made light of my empty stomach and tired body.

I didn't skulk about. I went home to take my medicine. What was a whipping compared to a day with the hounds? My two dogs met me about a mile from the house. I knew by their big melancholy eyes that they were sorry for me. After jumping and frisking about and licking my hands, they dropped behind me at a safe distance. It was never a happy time for them while I was getting punished, for we shared each other's crimes. So I got my whipping, and one that I have never forgotten. Even supper, saved for me, could not heal my sense of aching injuries, in spite of all the plenty of the Irish way of living in those years. However, I was consoled by the thought that I should soon be a man. In fact, not long after, when my father attempted to beat me one day, I warned him that I was unwilling to be punished again, and that if he tried to, he would do it at his own risk. That was the last.

As I went into the schoolhouse next day I could hear the boys whisper:

"He's going to get it to-day."

They were right. I did get it. I entered the room as innocently as a kindergarten child. I noticed that the master, as he looked at me, swelled out venomously, and buttoned up his frock-tailed coat. But everything went well until roll-call, and I had hopes that he had given me up as a bad job. I was sadly mistaken. He called my name.

"Present, sir," I answered quite loudly.

"Come up here to the desk," he roared.

Then I knew that the price of the hunt had to be paid. He called the school to attention, and fixing his hateful eyes on me he blustered:

"I'm going to make an example of you. I'm going to teach you that I am master here and have to be obeyed." His frame shook with the anger he had been holding in leash a whole day. "You'll never amount to anything," he now roared, "you—you—you——"

I had a bitter enemy in school—Thomas Coulter by name. I could hear him snigger behind his hands. The master stepped down from his desk with the cane in his hands.

"Hold out your hand!" he shouted. "Twelve slaps with the cane for you!"

Four were considered a serious punishment, but twelve were out of the question. I held out my hands and took six—three on each. The welts were too painful for any more. When I refused and said that I had had enough, he sprang at me like a tiger and knocked me down, put his knee on my chest, and almost drove the wind out of me. Then he lost control of his temper completely, and beat me unmercifully. As I lay there on the schoolroom floor groaning with pain, he stood over me like a madman. Then realizing that he had done his job, he helped himself to a glass of water and resumed the work of the school.

I crawled to my seat, but not like a whipped cur by any means: rather with the determination to get even with that black-eyed brute. Half an hour later my chance came. I grabbed a glass ink-bottle, and being good at throwing cobble-stones, I struck him over the eye, laying bare the bone.

With blood dripping down his shirt, he tumbled from his high-topped desk to the platform. I, weak and bruised, feeling that my job was done, but sick at the sight of it, crawled out of the school and staggered home.

I was not sent to that school again.

The parish people were terribly upset over my crime, but never a word did they say against the schoolmaster for what he had done to me. Strange to say, my father openly took my side. He was willing to abuse me himself, but when it came to public punishment, I at once became a son of his, and as such was entitled to consideration. My mother, being the village diplomat, had to smooth the troubled waters, which she was well qualified to do.

CHAPTER THREE

CONQUESTS

I was sent to another school in another village, but my time there was short also, for the hounds and the huntsmen passed that way too, and I had learned nothing from my former experience. I rode a donkey to and from that school. The distance was far, although you could count the Irish miles on three fingers of the left hand.

One afternoon I was coming home feeling very happy. I had been promoted to a higher grade and was beginning to like the school. My young enemy of the other school, Thomas Coulter, who had laughed when the master whipped me, was also riding a donkey that afternoon. The two animals met in the road, head on. They stopped and exchanged sniffs of greeting. Thomas and I growled at each other like two strange bulldogs, and without a word dismounted, pulled off our coats, and flew at each other's throats.

Thomas was older and heavier, and, as usual, he blackened both my eyes and made my nose bleed. I rode home, horrible to look at. My mother bathed my face and washed the blood off, saying in her gallant way:

"Oh, how I wish that sometime you could whip that boy!"

She cooked me two eggs and had me drink a pitcher of fresh buttermilk. Then she asked me where Thomas was. I told her up by the Four Roads. I knew that she wanted me to go back and see if I couldn't even the score. Mother was prudent, but her thoughts spoke louder than her words.

"Go out to the bog," said she, "and bring me four leeches. I must have your eyes fixed up before school to-morrow."

I didn't go near the bogs. Up to the Four Corners I strode and met Thomas, the boss of the village boys.

"Come on," I said, "I'm going to whip you this time."

He was whipped, and well whipped. I have often wondered since whether my success was due to the eggs and the buttermilk, or to my mother's daring words: "I wish that sometime you could whip that boy!"

When I was twelve years old I had a childish fondness for girls of my age. I liked to be with them, to play with them, caress them, and—which often happened—to fight with them.

One girl in particular, Anne Bailey, I was very fond of. Dressed in starched apron and polished shoes, she would meet me at the stile and swing with me on the gate. I would carry her books home from school, and fight her fights—which were many. Anne, for a child of thirteen years, had a terrible temper. Few boys in the village had any use for her. I liked her because she fought for what she thought was right. The smaller children always had a square deal where Anne was concerned, even if she had to trim a boy to get it.

My admiration for her grew, I suppose, out of the fact that she never lost a fight. If she got into a tight place where she couldn't win with her fists, she would resort to cobble-stones, and Anne could throw those grey granite ragged stones, so common on the country roads in Ireland, with unerring accuracy. Her enemies would run before her for the cover of the hawthorn hedges. Yet she had characteristics that belong to her sex. She admired well-dressed boys. On Sunday mornings she would give me her most coquettish smile, for then I was togged in my best.

When I was fifteen, mother had me join a band, and while I remained at home I learned to play the cornet, clarionet, and flute. Music may provide to the imaginative the pleasures of winged flight through starry spaces. In me, perhaps because I was over-imaginative, music wrought agonies of longing. Rainbow-tinted, velvet harmonies, of sights and sounds beyond my ken—over there—north, south, east and west : over beyond the sea. Oceans of colour to cross in that winged ship, flitting through the gauzy ether, and wonder-lands would rise up on the horizon . . .

I often think of the bandmaster, and how different

he was from my first schoolmaster. What a sense of humour he had, and what pains he took to teach me! What long rides he took on his old white mule! He came on Thursday evenings. His breath smelled strongly of whisky, but his teaching was none the worse on that account.

Our maids at home had been with us so long that they were part of the household. Only the dairy-maid was changed from time to time, for her position seemed to be one that inevitably led to matrimony. On these occasions there would be a great discussion as to the next one to fill her place. But Maggie, the cook, never changed. She had been with us for years and years. She ruled our goings-out and our comings-in, and woe betide us if we did not do justice to the good things that were set before us: no mean task, when one considers the three hearty meals and the three between-meals that punctuated the Irish farmer's day.

Maggie thought a great deal of the music-master: perhaps because he was good to me, who was her prime favourite; perhaps because he ate unsparingly of everything she placed before him on those hungry Thursday nights; perhaps because her soul was also full of music, surcharged with the ceaseless din of pots and pans.

The bandmaster was always kind and smiling, and made light of our mistakes, while he stuck his fingers in his ears most comically, to listen for discords, he said. For the life of me I could not see how that process could sharpen his perceptions, but he seemed to locate unpleasant sounds with unerring accuracy.

He had a difficult task to teach us country boys to play together, but he did, and rode his mule over twenty miles of cobble-stones once a week to do it. How excited and happy the old fellow was when at last, after four months of practice and effort, we played "The Minstrel Boy" without a hitch! That was his favourite piece, and he felt that if a band could play that, it could master the world of music.

Many years ago he and the old mule have gone up the Long Trail to return no more. Only in an occasional thought, like the memory of spring-time, do they return—the mule and the music-master.

CHAPTER FOUR

OFF TO SEA

Long before I was seventeen I had some knowledge of the sea. Often I had sailed away in an open boat out of sight of land, and again many coastwise schooners put into the Lough. I had learned to run aloft, and knew many of the sails and ropes—in fact I was about ready to leave home and sail away. Yet my mother held me for another year, hoping vainly to keep me to a course at the University. But school I detested, and judging from my changes, school detested me. Father thought that he might be able to make a farmer of me. Mother, in spite of her intellectual yearnings, knew differently. She knew that the wild waves and the flapping canvas called me, and that my harvest waited for me in the deep sea.

Winter was over that year, and I was nearing my eighteenth birthday, which was near Saint Patrick's Day (the one day in the year when my father permitted himself to celebrate until he could celebrate no more). The farmers were ploughing the fields, and the hawthorn buds were bursting with coming spring. The wild birds were mating and starting to build their nests, and the lark, never forgetful of his praise of the spring, sang his song way up in the sky.

My two dogs were old now. Prince seldom hunted with me in the bogs, and when one stayed behind, the other did too. I loved them and hated to leave them. We had shared a great deal together, especially Prince and I; our joys and sorrows had been many. But now he was old and stiff, and I felt that if he should go with me, it would only be for a little while. He was soon to rove with the dogs who had gone on before him, in the valleys where deer and duck and hare are plentiful, and dogs' barks are but memories of their yesterdays.

Mother saw to my going away. She packed my clothes, socks and pulse-heaters. These last were a large part of her creed. One would be immune to any epidemic if they were worn on the wrists. I took them to please her, although my vocation, above all others, called not for pulse-warming. Then she tucked some money in my pocket. I kissed her good-bye, and waved from the hill.

I can see her now, gathering up her white apron to wipe the tears away, a picture of love and self-sacrifice. My father, I am now ashamed to say, I did not see. What he said to my mother I can readily guess, for I never saw nor heard from him again.

When I said good-bye to Irish Anne, tears like dew-drops, the kind that cluster on a spider's web in the early morning, shone in her big blue eyes. She was nearly a woman then, and religiously inclined. Her days of cobble-stone throwing were over. We parted with friendship's kiss. I learned years after that she was married and had a large family of boys and girls. Perhaps I may have met some of her children in the highways of my rambles, but how was I to know them?

The night boat for Glasgow used to make the trip in about twelve hours. I took it and landed in Glasgow the following morning, going straight, with a sailor's instinct, to a sailors' boarding-house. It was on the Broomielaw.

A Swede ran it. He was married to a Highland woman, and together they made the Scandinavian sailors' boarding-house hum. He was a drunkard who had formerly been bosun on a Black Ball liner. She was endowed with Scotch thrift combined with business sense, and ever had an eye open for a "homeward bounder," with his pocket full of money. Such a one would always be welcomed to the head of her table.

The Swede had my pay for one month's board, and assured me a ship by that time. Seeing that I had some money left still, he urged me to put it in his care. Like the young fool that I was, I turned it over to him, and of course that was the last of my money. He went out promptly and spent it all on a glorious drunk.

The boarding-house catered to all creeds and colours; everyone was on an equal footing. When one sang, all sang. In a fight everybody joined in, and after the fight, when the broken pieces were swept away and the scalp wounds had been plastered, they would all drink together and be friends again.

When I had been there a couple of weeks, the Swede asked me if I would go with him down the Clyde on a sloop he had, to a place called Broderick. He wanted to load her with sand to haul back and sell at Glasgow. Then he would give me back the money he had taken from me. Once more I "fell" for him, and went along, on a short but perilous trip that was to bring me within plain sight of Davy Jones's locker.

CHAPTER FIVE

MY FIRST VOYAGE

SHE was a sloop of about thirty tons. Her one mast was stuck forward and her main boom was about thirty-five feet long. The sails were old and many times patched. The small cabin aft was filthy and full of rats. The deck was so old that you could see through the seams, and young as I was, I was fully aware of the risk I was taking, sailing in her. But knowing that the Clyde never got very rough, and believing that I should get back my five pounds, I felt like taking a chance.

So one morning we set sail: myself, another penniless sailor, and the proprietor of the Scandinavian sailors' boarding-house, late bosun of a Black Ball liner.

The Swede wasn't much of a sloop sailor. I could see that by the way he handled her. Between drifting and sailing we made Greenock, eighteen miles below Glasgow. Here he put in, saying that he needed water. But it was whisky he wanted. He sold practically everything that was movable on deck to a junk man. He did leave an anchor on board. Then for two more days he drank up the

MY FIRST VOYAGE

junk money, while the other sailor and I stayed on board and waited.

On the morning of the third day he came aboard broke and sick, and we set sail again for Broderick. We made it in twenty-four hours, that is, we made the beach where the sand was, and dropped the anchor a quarter of a mile from the surf. We put the boat over and commenced taking on sand by the simple process of loading the small boat, rowing off, and shovelling the sand into the sloop.

We had more than half loaded her when the Swede rushed out one morning, shouting that we were caught in a storm.

"Hurry, boys," he called, "get the mainsail on her!"

It was a storm sure enough, but not a bad one just then. There was a good breeze coming from the south-west, and with it a long ground swell. The Swede was pale with fear. The sloop was on a lee shore and he didn't know how to beat her off. We set the mainsail and started to heave up the anchor.

I told him that was not the way to get off a lee shore. The old Irish fishermen had taught me how it was done in their fishing-smacks. Shoot up the jib, slip the cable, give her the mainsail, and away, close hauled, to fight for sea room until you get a good lead off shore. But the Swedish bosun would not listen to a boy.

She started to drag her anchor and was headed straight for a spit of rocks. As she dragged, he prayed, then started to swear, and said he wouldn't give a damn if only the sloop belonged to him.

"Who does she belong to?" I shouted, as we were nearing the rocks.

"My wife and brother-in-law," he cried, and with death staring us in the face he went on to tell me how she happened to be theirs. I forget the intricacies of the ownership at this distance, but I can still hear the shrill notes of his high-pitched voice rising trivially above the solemn tones of nature. Before he finished, however, I felt that the grave would be preferable to an interview with his wife, once the sloop was lost.

She struck the rocks. The mast went overboard and the sea lashed over her. The undertow would pull away from the rocks only to get a good start with the next sea. Slam, she'd go. We clung to her like leeches, the Swede crying in bitter anguish:

"I wouldn't give a damn if she belonged to me— I wouldn't give a damn——"

Young and fearless as I was, I had but little hope that any of us would get off with our lives.

The sloop gave a hard thump, and the sternpost was sprung from its rusty fastenings and floated alongside. Another sea like the last one and she would smash into firewood, while the bosun of the Black Ball liner and his crew would be found bloated and bruised on the high-water line.

But the God of the Deep was not ready as yet to destroy my dream of the sea. I was to find worse than this before he was through with me. The

MY FIRST VOYAGE

sloop, what was left of her, by some strange freak of the waves, swung through head on, with the jibboom reaching over the rocks. The sailor was quick to seize this Heaven-sent opportunity. He crawled out on the jibboom end, and when the sea lurched back, dropped to the sloppy rock, and safety.

I wasn't so fortunate. When I let go the jibboom the undertow caught me and I got pretty badly mauled—a cut head, skinned shins, a few sore ribs —and I was gorged full of salt water.

The Swede was doomed; that seemed a foregone conclusion. We were powerless to help him, and the thought made me cold with horror. Years afterwards, hundreds of miles from land, I saw men drown within sight of a ship, and felt the same overpowering sense of helpless misery.

But the Swede was destined to live, and drink his ale out of his pewter mugs, and watch where the homeward bounder hung his trousers. While I looked, with my thoughts going heavenwards, a sea struck the sloop and she broke in two. I turned my head away, for I couldn't watch a human being drown. Then a curious thing happened. A short distance to the right of the spot where the sloop was pounding against the rocks lay a small sand-patch between two reefs. It wasn't over twenty feet wide, and here the waves swept high on the sandy beach. The Swede still clung to the cabin hatch, and now that part of the sloop was carried out and away from the rocks, and washed high and dry upon the patch of sandy strand. He was none the worse, aside from being soaked, while I was bruised and bleeding.

Some time later the life-savers came, and with them a dignified, portly man, the wreckmaster. Very important he was. As we stood there shivering, wet and cold, with not a shilling among us, the world looked dark enough. Then I remembered what my father had once said:

"If he goes to sea, he'll soon come home again."

The thought put fresh pep into me.

CHAPTER SIX

JILTED

There's a bit of silver lining to nearly every dark cloud. Strolling down the beach, and heading for the wreck, came an Englishman. He looked warm and comfortable in his Scotch tweeds and long homespun stockings.

The Swede and the wreckmaster were busy over the salvage question, so I told the Englishman about the wreck and how we had managed to save ourselves. He proved his genuine interest and sympathy by putting his hand into his pocket and handing me a gold sovereign. My, but that coin looked good to me!

The Swede's ear, ever attuned, caught the jingle, and he wanted me to share it with him.

"Oh, no," said I, "every dog for himself now. I'm through with you."

That much, at least, experience had taught me.

Someone paid the sailor's fare and mine back to Glasgow, maybe the wreckmaster, in lieu of paying or the wreck. The Swede stayed behind, either to attend to business, as he said, or because he was afraid to face his wife.

Why the sailor and I went back to the boarding-house on the Broomielaw, is a question for psychologists to answer. It is something I never have understood, any more than I can understand why other sailors constantly did the same thing: returning persistently to places where they were sure to be robbed and abused.

Back we went, and the reception that we were given by the Swede's wife and her brother is one to be remembered. The news of the wreck had reached Glasgow ahead of us, and when I walked into the boarding-house she knocked me down. When I got up, she knocked me down again. It seemed that I was the cause of the disaster, in that I had given her husband my money.

Then came the turn of the sailor boarders. They voiced their opinion of the greenhorn sailor. The great trouble, it seemed, was that the sloop was not insured—as if I was responsible for that. The blame was on me, fully.

I made up my mind that night that if I was to become a sailor I should have also to become a fighter, because I could see that without this qualification one could never be a success on the high seas.

The trail of my next venture did not take me out of the Swede sailors' boarding-house, but led me toward the portals of romance, nevertheless. Jessie, the waitress who served the meals, seemed to admire me, or perhaps it was the suits I wore. She was the usual type of seaport girl, but to me quite a new sort. She admired new faces and dressy young

JILTED

men. While she led me to believe I was her first choice, she was madly in love with a fireman on a steamer. He was to arrive home shortly from a Mediterranean port, and I was to find out where I stood with the giddy Scotch lassie.

When he arrived he came to the boarding-house in his go-ashore clothes. Tall and lanky he was, and baked white from the heat of the stokehole. The coal-dust was still in his ears, and his eyelashes were cemented black from the slack of the slag. His eyes were small and glassy, and there was a vicious look about him as he rolled into the boarding-house and demanded to know where his Jessie was. She was not there just then, so he bought a pitcher of beer and sat down to drink and talk with the other sailors. They, being creative gossips, and ready to humour and cater to the homeward bounder, told him of the faithlessness of his Jessie : how she seemed to be very much in love with another man, and how they doubted by this time if she had any regard for him at all.

"Who is he?" he cried, and I trembled where I sat, at the sight of his gnarly fists.

But I need not have been afraid. No danger that they would betray me. Agreeable as a fight always was to them, beer was more agreeable still, and a homeward bounder silenced is a homeward bounder lost for ever. They dodged the question.

He became very angry and swore that women were all alike and not to be trusted. He bought more beer all around, to the satisfaction of the sailors, while he gulped his down with oaths of revenge.

"I'll show her she can't fool with my bloody 'eart!" he shouted.

Just then the door to the dining-room opened, and Jessie walked in. She exclaimed, as she ran toward him, "Ah, me bright laddie's home at last!"

"Keep away from me, Jessie," he stuttered. "I've been 'earing about you since I've been away. Now I'm going to get me another girl."

Jessie appeared crushed, crying: "Oh, Harry, don't leave me like this! I have been true to you."

"By God, you're a liar! It's off between you and me!" declared Harry. Waving her aside, he got up from the table with the gesture of an outraged hero.

Then like a story-book heroine, Jessie screamed at the top of her voice that if he did this she would drown herself in the Clyde.

"Go to it!" cried Harry as he staggered out of the boarding-house.

True to her instinct, she started out of the house shrieking, and ran, with hair flying in the breeze, across the street to the Clyde's rim. The sailors ran after her out of the boarding-house, shouting and urging the bystanders not to "let 'er drown 'er bloomin' self." I ran with them, and Harry ran too.

Barefooted women with children in arms joined the chase, as well as a couple of pedlars, who dropped their packs and wrung their hands as they ran

JILTED

to the Clyde. A longshoreman was there, coiling down rope on the wharf. He alone appeared undisturbed as he stopped flaking it long enough to speak to Jessie.

"Well, lass, you're at it again! Who is it this time?"

Jessie stopped before this stringer at the bottom of the wharf.

"I'm going over this time," she cried vengefully, "and no mistake!"

"Over ye go then, I'll no stop ye," and he smiled to himself.

"Stop, Jessie, don't jump over!" The conscience-smitten, ale-laden fireman thrust his way up to her and took her in his arms.

The longshoreman grinned boldly and went on coiling down his rope. The sentimental boarding-house sailors swallowed hard as if they were eating sea biscuit. The pedlars walked back to their packs with their hands behind their backs, while the mothers gave their babies the breast and wondered what it was all about. I slunk away to where the broken shadows from the tall ships humped over the hydraulic capstans.

This was the Glasgow I knew in those days, and a fitting place for the jilt of a green, gawky country boy by a fickle boarding-house waitress. My romance of that period ended there. There were many more, and doubtless, if I can remember them all, I shall touch on them as I rove along.

CHAPTER SEVEN

LIVERPOOL JACK

THERE happened to be a Blue-nose ship sailing in a few days, and the Swede's wife considered this a good chance to get rid of me. So I was shipped aboard the Blue-nose barque, bound for Sidney, Cape Breton. I wrote to my mother and told her that at last I was off to sea. There was a cheap outfitting store next to the boarding-house, and here I was equipped from my month's advance. They took it all, and gave me a blanket, a straw tick, a few cigars that I couldn't smoke, a clammy handshake, and this God-speed: " Be sure and visit us again." This was part of their stock-in-trade. Hell will never close its gates as long as one of these outfitting stores continues to exist.

We towed down the Clyde on the Blue-nose barque. The crew was a conglomeration of everything: Greeks, Scandinavians, English, Irish, Scotch, Germans, and negroes. The mate was over six feet tall; stout but agile, with a hand on him that had the spread of a mallard duck's wing, and a moustache that hid his mouth. His voice would chill you to the marrow, and he was proud of it.

The captain was broad and porky. He carried his wife and child along. She was quite the reverse of him in looks: tall and slender as a bean-pole. The child, a boy, was three years old, and able to run around the poop deck.

When we got well out to sea we set all sail and let the tug boat go. At first I was of little use on board that ship. I knew nothing about square riggers. But I was soon to learn.

About the second day out, everyone commenced to scratch himself. The child too would lean against the binnacle and scratch his little back. The Blue-nose barque was lousy fore and aft, and we even came upon vermin crawling in the upper topsails. One old sailor, who had many seafaring years behind him, remarked that, as nearly as he could remember, the flying jibboom was the highest he had ever caught them on a ship.

Sailors as a rule in those days were clean. They took baths and scrubbed their clothes. The crew of our barque got busy, but while we drove the vermin from the decks and forecastle, we were never sure about the sails. They were never changed while I was aboard her.

The food was new to me: stirabout, stewed apples and gingerbread; salt horse—rather scarce —and pork once a week on pea-soup day. The hardtack, the boss of the forecastle said, was good. He was a Liverpool sailor, and the biscuits were supposed to have come from there.

No one in the forecastle dared question his statements. He was a fighter, and we had a world of respect for him. His word was law to the shellbacks. Four days out from Glasgow, a heavy-set Dane thought that he would become boss of the forecastle. The quarrel arose over the equal distribution of the gingerbread. The Dane was a big eater, and a greedy one.

Liverpool Jack, that was his name, had his code of ethics: all were to have an equal share of the food. The Dane was the more powerful man of the two, and he provoked a fight.

They stripped to the waist for action. We cleared the benches away to give them room. The forecastle was large, which favoured Jack. In all the years I spent on the sea, I never saw another to equal that fight on the Blue-nose barque. Jack beat the Dane and trimmed him until he cried quits. The fight was clean and speedy. There was no hitting nor kicking when one of them was down. The Dane's head was large before the fight—but who can describe how large it was after? We led him around for a few days, and he became quite a good Dane, satisfied with his equal share of the gingerbread.

While I was always doing the wrong thing from a seamanship point of view, I got along very well with the sailors in the forecastle. But not with the mate, who seemed to despise me. I had told him that I was a sailor, and he had found out that I was only a green country boy.

One evening as we were nearing the eastern

edge of the Newfoundland Banks it commenced to blow. The mate ordered the main royal clewed up. The barque carried no fore royal. The breeze was too strong for this light sail. Usually it took two men to furl it, but this evening he shouted to me to shin up and make it fast alone.

I did get a gasket around it, but I was unable to pull the sail up on the yard the way it should have been, snugly furled. When I came down on deck again it was growing dark. The mate greeted me with an oath and a kick from his Wellington boots.

"Get up there," he roared, "and get that sail up on the yard, or I'll break every bone in your body!"

I have often thought of that kick. It sent me aloft again to be with the stars. That night was the first in my life that I felt really alone with them. The barque below me looked like a helpless bug being borne away by the whim of the sea. The light from the binnacle lamp shone on the figure of the helmsman. What an insignificant figure he looked! The very wheel looked like a spider's web, spun for the moths of frail humanity.

The mate had made me angry, and I was in no hurry to obey him. As I looked at the stars above me and the restless sea below, I felt that it was worth more than one kick to be allowed the privilege of being alone with one's self on the main royal of a Blue-nose barque in the fine thrill of such a night as this. Feeling so, the strength of youth aided me to the difficult task, and I rolled the sail up on the yard. The mate might abuse me, but he could never destroy my love for the sea.

One day we had an accident that brought gloom to the forecastle. A Greek sailor fell through the 'tween decks down into the lower hold. We carried him up to the deck. He was unconscious from a blow on the head. He had the bunk over me, and we put him into it. The mate came forward with liniment and orders to rub his head.

"And," said he, "give him these pills when he comes to."

Beecham's pills for a fractured skull! Such was the practice of medicine aboard the average sailing ship of those days.

The Greek sailor didn't come to for forty-eight hours, and in the meantime our Scotch cook, out of kindness of heart, prepared a flax-seed poultice for the head and claimed the honour of restoring the Greek to his senses again.

Sailors were hard to kill thirty years ago, barring an accident, such as drowning or falling from aloft. They were a good deal like the jackass —they would grow so old that they would just wander away and die from old age.

The sailors of to-day are better fed and clothed, they have rooms to sleep in, and waiters to serve their food. But to-day there are no chanties sung, and sailors go around with long-drawn faces; when they have to pull a rope they might as well be landlubbers—there's not a chirrup out of them. Neither do they seem to see the sunset or the stars. It's sleep they want, with their eight hours on and their sixteen hours off. "Sissies," the calloused old-timers call them.

Twenty-three days out from Glasgow we sailed into Cape Breton harbour and dropped the anchor. I may mention here that the barque was in ballast from Scotland. We received orders at Cape Breton to take on more ballast and to proceed to the St. Lawrence River, and thence to the mouth of the Saguenay. There she was to load lumber for a South American port.

Reports came to us that yellow fever was raging in South America. Liverpool Jack announced it to the forecastle, with the declaration that *he* was not going to any yellow-fever port.

We sailed up the St. Lawrence to the saw-mill town and anchored about two miles from the beach. The lumber came off in barges. We took it aboard through the 'tween-deck ports, and stowed it down in the hold.

There was no possible chance that I could see to get ashore, and I was as anxious as Jack to leave the barque. The stories the crew told in the forecastle had me badly scared. One old man was saying:

"I'll tell you men how it is down there. You come to anchor in Rio harbour at night, and if the wind should haul off the land and blow from the city, you're dead in the morning. Mind you," with warning hand upraised, " that's not all, men. You turn as black as hell," he whispered.

That story was enough for me. There wouldn't be any escape from Rio. It sounded worse than hell.

CHAPTER EIGHT

AN ESCAPE

THE captain and the mate were seeing to it that the crew should not get away. It always mystified me how swiftly and unerringly the most secret and closely guarded news reached the "Old Man." When the time came that I myself occupied that envied post, it seemed more mysterious still if anything escaped my watchfulness and perception. So far does one advance in the sense of responsibility as he earns the stages of promotion from the forecastle to the poop deck.

The captain's boat was hoisted on board every evening, and the oars put away. There was also a night watchman with two guns strapped around him, yet he did not seem so very fierce. Being a Frenchman, and rather religious, I doubted if the necessity could arise to make him shoot to kill.

Liverpool Jack and I held a conference and decided that the time was near to make a dash for freedom. The barque would be loaded in a few days, and then it would be too late. The watchman did not speak English. At this Jack was quite upset, because he could not speak French. So was he deprived of a medium for diplomatic manœuvring.

The watchman had a birch-bark canoe in which he paddled to the ship in the evening, leaving it tied at the stern of a lighter of lumber. We saw it, and kept our discovery from the crew, who were also trying to devise some means of getting ashore.

Liverpool Jack was as crafty as a sea otter. One night he called me, about twelve o'clock. I had been working late and was sleeping soundly after whittling a toy for the captain's boy, for I have always been fond of children.

" Roll up a suit of clothes in your oilskin coat," said he. " We're going to-night. I've had my eye on the watchman."

" You're not going to kill him ? " I asked, faltering a little as I scrawled the child's name on a scrap of paper and left the toy in my bunk.

" Oh, no," reassured Jack, rather flattered. " We haven't time for that."

" Here's my plan," he whispered, " tie the bundle on your back and strip naked—we may have to swim for it. When the watchman walks over to the port side we'll slide down the rope hanging from the starboard bow, swim to the lighter, board her, creep over the lumber to the stern, and if all goes well, everything else is simple enough. Drop into the canoe and paddle ashore. Then we can hide in the woods."

It all seemed simple enough to him, but I felt as

if the last of my time on earth had come. " Suppose they kill us ! " I objected.

He looked me over quickly, as if he had half a mind to leave me there and then. But his eye softened, and I knew that he had in a way grown fond of me. He answered, roughly enough :

" How about Rio ! It's pretty damned brave you'll have to learn to be, my boy, if you mean to stay away from your mother."

All ready, naked, with our bundles strapped on our backs, we stood forward of the galley, both our eyes on the watchman. It was in the month of June, when daylight comes early in those latitudes. Already the ship's bells had told one o'clock. Surely the devil possessed the Frenchman. He was not making a move to cross to the port side. Where he stood now, at the starboard side, he commanded a full view of lighter and canoe. I could see him toying with his revolver and peering suspiciously from time to time into the forecastle. How we had managed to come up without his seeing us was a mystery.

We waited till past two, still nervously watching for the Frenchman to move. Mars hung low in the eastern sky blinking in the dawn. This was my first big adventure, and while thoroughly scared, I still had to admire cool-headed Liverpool Jack.

" Let's go," he whispered with compelling determination. " We won't wait another minute. The damned Frenchman's either frozen to the deck, or asleep."

We lowered ourselves cautiously over the bow, into the water. Oh, but it was cold, and there were two miles to swim to the beach. He took the lead and headed for the lighter, which we boarded. Just as we started to crawl over the lumber, the Frenchman spied us. He raised his voice in a roaring torrent of choking, snorting French. Then he fired his revolver, and the echoes awoke the cranes on the strand.

Jack paid no attention to this, but with me following him closely, kept on for the stern of the lighter. He got into the canoe all right. I had never been in one. It was birch-bark, and in my haste I jumped on to it and turned it over, spilling us both into the water. The current was strong under the stern of the barque, and when we got our bearings we were well away from the ship. But as we rose, they saw us.

Bullets began to splash around us, and I could hear the mate's voice heading the outcry. "Dive!" panted Jack, and suited the action to the word. I tried to, but couldn't on account of the oilskin pack. Soon, however, the current took us out of range and they began to lower a boat. Presently our feet struck the bottom of the sandy beach, and we saw, in the early morning light, the captain's boat heading for the shore.

Naked we landed, and naked we ran for at least five miles into the woods. When we stopped the sun was up, and the mosquitoes were flocking by the million, ready to feast upon two runaway sailors.

AN ESCAPE

We put on our clothes wet as they were, and lay down to go to sleep. But the mosquitoes saw to it that we did not sleep long. When we awoke we were hungry and stiff. Not a penny did either of us have to buy something to eat. This thought gave no concern to Jack.

"I'll go and get some grub," he said. "I know enough French to ask for it."

He took a trail that led to the saw-mill town, and when he came back he had news and food—two loaves of bread, a pail of buttermilk, and a chunk of butter.

"I heard that the watchman got fired," he mumbled between bites, "and that the mate is still looking for us."

CHAPTER NINE

BUGABOO

"HAVE you any more news?" said I after a while, for Jack was looking back persistently over his shoulder, and it seemed to me that danger lurked in the trees, and that the burly mate must by now be hot on our trail. Yet I was enjoying this taste of a freedom I had never known before—freedom to roam regardless of God or man.

"Yes, I have more news," said Jack. "We follow a trail that leads to the right, and forty miles from here we come to a river. There we can take a boat and go up the Saguenay to Chicoutimi."

"But," I objected, "how are we going to take a passenger boat? We have no money."

"Leave that to me," said he, "I've been in tighter places than this before, and got out of them too."

By now I had full faith in Jack, and I believed he could do anything he set out after. Optimistic he ever was, and never without a smile or an encouraging word, and yet ready to fight at the drop of the hat. We filled ourselves full of bread and buttermilk, for we had no assurance when we should eat again. Then we stuffed what was left of the bread into our pockets and started out, heading as directed through the Canadian woods, without guide, or milepost or sidelight.

We walked until it grew dark, not knowing if we were on the right trail, and Jack not caring. We came to an old log bunkhouse, and crawled into pine-needle bunks. But not for long, thanks to my foolishness.

When we lay down to sleep Jack cautioned against mosquitoes. We wrapped our coats about our heads in the hope of keeping our faces and necks clear. Jack could adapt himself to anything, and in less than five minutes he was asleep. I would have smothered with a coat around my head, and being sleepless I stood looking out of the window. Presently I thought I saw lights moving all around in the forest.

"The mate! the mate!" I cried, tugging at Jack in a frenzy of fear.

"Where?" he asked sleepily, yet alert and not at all dismayed.

"See the lights?" Truly by now there were a dozen of them, it seemed to me.

"Come on," said he, "this is not the place for us." He grabbed his coat and ran out of the bunkhouse door, with me after him. We had no sense of the direction we took, but we ran until we could run no farther.

"I guess they'll have a job overhauling us now," panted Jack as he stopped.

"Yes," I agreed, "we've gone a long way, if only we've gone straight."

Many a laugh I've had over that chase. While we were sitting there, exhausted from the run, I saw the lights again.

"Heavens, there they are again, there they come!" I cried, jumping up. Jack, being somewhat infected with my state of mind, jumped too.

"Where in hell do you see those lights?"

"There! There!"

"Great God!" roared Jack. "They're not lights. They're fireflies."

I didn't know what fireflies were, but they carried their lights with them, and they looked like masthead lights to me.

We fought mosquitoes until daylight broke. Then, damp, cold, and hungry, we continued along the trail. There were many trails: which one led to the steamboat landing, only God knew. We walked on. Noon came and went, and our trouble now lay, not in the distance to the river, but in our empty stomachs. Hunger, the great disciplinarian, wished us back to the Blue-nose barque. Ah! We mourned gingerbread and stewed apples, yes, and almost Rio and the yellow fever. The more we talked, the hungrier we grew.

Jack became silent, and I, who had never known hunger, staggered on behind him. It was late in the afternoon when we came to an opening and saw a house in the distance.

"Come on, we're all right now," said Jack.

They gave us plenty to eat at that house and showed us to the boat-landing. Some people are indeed kind. An old French lady met us at the door. She could not understand our English, but she could read our faces, and that was enough for the dear old soul. She welcomed us with the warmth of a mother heart. Her house was our house, and Jack, who should have been calloused by his years of beach-combing, bowed his head, while a tear or two dropped on the plate before him.

It was one o'clock in the morning when the boat made the landing. How we were to get aboard without paying a fare I did not know, and Jack would not say. He did suggest that I follow him.

"Haul in the gang-plank!" the mate shouted.

I stood trembling behind a pile, afraid to be seen. The gang-plank was in, the boat moving. Then like a flash, Jack cried:

"Take a run and a jump and board her!"

He who seeks adventure must put fear behind him. We boarded the moving steamer, and hid away in the lee shadows of the smoke-stack. We were unseen because the crew, when they took in the gangway, moved forward, and the night hid us from the eyes on the bridge.

I had learned more in two days than in all the eighteen years I had lived.

CHAPTER TEN

A COURAGEOUS CAPTAIN

As the boat rounded the bends in that beautiful river, and the chug-chug of the engines echoed back from the granite walls that guarded the water in its peaceful flow to the sea, I curled up by the warm smoke-stack, and unheeding the morrow, fell asleep.

When I awoke the sun was high, the boat was moored to the wharf and the sound of winches greeted my ear.

"Come on, Jack," I said, "this must be Chicoutimi." We walked ashore. No one on board noticed us.

Chicoutimi as we saw it was a good-sized town, and a railroad was being built from there to Montreal. I hunted for work and secured a job painting steel bridges. Jack said that he was going on to Montreal to find another ship; he was a sailor and not a landlubber. No railroad work for him, climbing over steel bridges.

Whether there is in a sailor's make-up a certain amount of fatalism, or whether it is mere childish faith in the future, or whether sailors take their friendships so for granted that separation is not a matter of moment, certain it is that partings with them are over in a minute, and equally certain that, given the usual course of events, they will sometime meet again. Of all my shipmates, few have I quitted for ever at the end of a voyage.

Jack said good-bye to me as he would to a comparative stranger, and started up the railroad track singing in his hearty voice the old-time chantey:

> " In Amsterdam there lived a maid,
> And she was mistress of her trade,
> No more I'll go a-roving with you, fair maid.
> A-ro-o-ving, a-ro-o-ving,
> Since roving's been my ru-u-in,
> I'll go no more a-ro-o-ving
> With you, fair maid."

He disappeared in the distance with never a backward look. The prospect of the two hundred and forty mile walk to Montreal meant nothing to him.

I was too young not to feel heart-broken at being left by the only real friend I had found since leaving home. Evidently, I thought, I didn't mean much to him; he might have understood the weariness which bound me to work now instead of following him. But I was mistaken in all this, for Jack's heart was of the warmest; I was to have proof enough when we met again.

For two months I painted bridges at one dollar and seventy-five cents a day, for as many hours as twice the eight-hour day. Neck-breaking work it was. Seventy-five cents went for board and room, the rest for clothes, and when I had paid my car fare to Quebec I had a little left over.

The call of the sea had me again, and I took the boat down the Saguenay, as passenger this time, and found a sailors' boarding-house at Quebec. An Irishwoman, three daughters and a son ran it. The food and treatment were better than in the Glasgow boarding-house, but everybody in it was either drunk or fighting most of the time. I have always been, as the tippler says, "able to drink a drop of beer now and then," but I have always had a horror of degenerating through drink. Where I got this feeling I do not know, for my actions as a young man were wild enough. My captains later on, when I sailed as first mate, would shake their heads over the irresponsibility of me ashore, while at sea they could sleep in peace when I had charge of the watch.

By the end of a week I had shipped aboard a square rigger bound for Liverpool and loaded with lumber. Here I was to learn another phase of the sea: the psychology of the men who command deep-water ships—and in a way I was to find myself.

The captain, an Irishman from County Wexford, was in the last throes of consumption. The mate was a burly Scotchman, and a drunkard. The second mate was old and rheumatic. The crew was mostly English. We had one negro sailor in the forecastle, born of an Irish father and a black mother in the

A COURAGEOUS CAPTAIN

West Indies, who, curiously enough, could speak only Gaelic. I was much excited and mystified by all this, for he was very black indeed; but the mate could understand him, and I soon found that I could too.

There were good men in the crew, and some excellent chantey men among them. They accepted me as a man, for now I stood as one: five feet ten, sinewy, quick of eye and hand, nimble on my feet, and deep-chested. Neither was I ill-looking nor ill-natured, being always quick to sympathize and quick to smile, although I was something of a fighter.

We towed down the St. Lawrence to the point where the river widened out, then made sail, and with a slanting breeze headed away for the Newfoundland Banks. The captain was constantly coughing and spitting, and in danger of dying before we reached Liverpool.

The mate ran out of whisky when we were two or three days out. He was in danger also, for he began to act like a crazy man. The cook, who was very vain, and always anxious to fascinate a pretty barmaid, carried with him some lotions and tonics to improve his good looks. The thirsty mate discovered this, and stole the cook's Florida water: three bottles of it. The perfumed water served as a substitute for whisky for a while.

A little Florida water seemed to improve his temper, and he gave his orders to the crew more sensibly, which relieved the strain in the forecastle.

The men were already superstitious : with the two chiefs afflicted, they figured that the ship was cursed, and that something was going to happen, for the scent of Florida was abroad in the air, enveloping the mate. And something did happen, as we were reaching away for the southern edge of the Banks.

One morning the captain staggered forward over the deckload of lumber and asked where the mate was. His voice was so weak that he could scarcely speak above a whisper; his eyes were sunken in his head, and he looked little better than a skeleton.

No one on board could find the mate. A sailor who had been aloft overhauling the fore upper topsail buntlines said that he hadn't seen the mate, but he had heard a splash alongside, in the middle watch. This settled the mystery. The mate had jumped overboard.

The next night we had a change of weather. The wind hauled to the south-east, and the sky turned black and stormy. The captain ordered all hands to take in sail, although there was not much wind to speak of. Not initiated yet to storms at sea, I revelled in this new adventure. I had become familiar with the ropes, yards and sails, and I was sure of my way about the ship. I could steer as well as anyone on board. Neither was I afraid of abuse nor punishment, for here was an altogether different atmosphere from that on the Blue-nose barque. But still more had I to learn.

A COURAGEOUS CAPTAIN

All the sails were furled to the lower topsails and the main upper topsail, so that the wooden square rigger lay wallowing in the trough of the sea, waiting and apparently helpless, without sails to drive her on. Later in the night, away to the south-east, the black clouds opened like the eye of some unearthly monster and an occasional star glimmered through.

"There comes the blasted gale!" shouted a sailor, and sure enough, a North Atlantic storm such as I have never seen, nor ever want to see again under the same conditions, closed in upon the ship with such squeezing, breathless rage, that it reeled her upon her beam ends and held her there in the storm-god's vice.

The captain, although gasping for the life that was soon to desert him, felt that he was good for one more fight with the elements, and, like the true sailor he was, he lashed himself to the weather rail of the poop deck, taking charge of the ship, the crew, and the night. Oh, how I longed to have the power to defy the wind and waves as he did! How courageous he looked, with the heavy, pounding seas roaring over him! With sunken eyes sparkling superhuman fire, he shouted out his orders fore and aft, between spasms of coughing. Never a thought he gave to his diseased, outworn body.

"Put your helm down!" he cried to me at the wheel.

When the gale struck the ship it caught her on the

beam. The yards were braced sharp on the port tack, and it seemed as though she'd never come up to the wind. The main upper topsail, bellied and stiff from the force of the gale, was pressing her down till the lee bulwark rail was under water. The captain's voice sounded again:

"Let the main upper topsail go by the run!"

As the yard came crashing down, the moaning and hissing wind in the rigging lent an uncanny feeling to the night. I trembled as I stood with my hands on the spokes of the wheel. My mind was alert to the peril and necessity of the hour, but there came momentary flashes when subconscious thoughts rose to the surface: thoughts of my mother, a composite picture of my early life, its desires and delights. I was ever an optimist, and the wish to get a full lading of life was uppermost in me then.

Still the wind raged, and still the old captain, lashed over there to windward of me, fought for his ship.

As the buntlines closed in on the topsail, the ship came slowly up into the wind. We were saved for the time being, but the seas kept coming higher. They washed the deckload of lumber overboard. One of the life-boats was carried away, and the other was in danger. We had only two boats left. A sailor commenced to swear, and I thought he'd never stop. He told us the "bloody old 'ooker's back" was "broke," and demanded of Heaven and

Hell what was to happen next. Towards daylight the sea was a mass of swirling foam, and the storm was growing worse.

Then we took in the fore and mizzen lower topsails, and hove her to under the main lower topsail. The captain stayed at his post, cautioning the man at the wheel from time to time. It was now nearly eight hours since he had taken this post, and he continued there without relief for hours more, while I, young and hardy, was grateful for relief and a cup of hot coffee at the end of two hours of awful strain at the wheel.

The carpenter's report, when he sounded the ship, was gloomy.

"Four feet of water in the hold, sir," I heard him tell the captain.

"Keep the pumps going, the storm will break shortly. It's just a little equinoctial disturbance." Then he told the steward to serve the men a glass of grog.

My opinion of men who command ships was formed then and there. I realized as fully as I do now, how little the world knows of these men, or of what they have given to spin the wheel of Progress.

We weathered the storm, and sunshine and blue skies were ours once again. The thought of a pay day, in Liverpool, and a trip home to see my mother, filled me with joy. Like all good sailors, I forgot the agonies we had passed through. The ship was waterlogged. Four hundred miles from Liverpool a western ocean steamer took us in tow and docked the ship for us without further trouble.

Strange to relate, the old captain lived until he had delivered the ship to her owners, and not much longer. He had to be taken in an ambulance to the hospital, where he died that day. Strange also to relate, the ship died too, for that very night the Queen's Dock caught fire, and she was destroyed.

There is a vague superstition among masters that it is not the best of luck to take out a ship whose previous master had her many years, and had died on the last voyage. However this may be, some years later I was offered the command of an old barquentine—the *Tam o' Shanter*, I think she was—whose master had just died. I accepted, put my things aboard, and then backed out for no reason except that I had such a feeling as many of us have experienced, that I should not go. Captain Donnelly took her, and his wife and two daughters went with him. They were never heard from again.

Although my pay for the voyage did not amount to much (three pounds, I think it was), I was in high glee, and about to take the night boat for Ireland, when I discovered that someone had stolen my money. I learned that it was one of my own shipmates. I was in a strange city without a penny. The men of the crew, lost in the city crowd, were of no help to me now. Oh, how I damned, and still damn, the sailor that steals from a shipmate! I couldn't go home, nor could I write for money, nor could I say that I was in Liverpool and wouldn't come home. I did what I thought best, and didn't write at all, so that mother would never know that I had been so close to her.

Once again I hunted up a sailors' boarding-house.

CHAPTER ELEVEN

THE LIME JUICER

THE pierhead sailors' boarding-house on Pike Street, known as Kelly's, was always open for hard-up sailors. There I went, and they took me to board with the stipulation that I would ship on anything that carried sail at a moment's notice. Like all the others, it was a starvation house; but if Mrs. Kelly liked you, she would give you a cup of tea in the afternoon. With meals it was first come, first served, as long as the spuds held out.

The sailors who stopped there were a miserable lot, starved-looking, with their clothes in tatters. It was only by merest chance that the master or mate of a ship would take any of them. Consequently, being a place of last resort, Kelly's came to be known as the "Pierhead Jump House." When a ship was about to sail short-handed, Kelly had his men lined up on the wharf, and the mate, not daring to sail without the necessary number of men, would hastily take his pick of the offerings.

I was one week at the boarding-house when my turn came for the pierhead jump. I had been hoping to get away, for I did not have the courage to write to my mother on account of my father's taunts; yet it was hard to stay here, so near home. The sea held no terrors for me now, and I loved it more than ever.

A Dundee ship, one of the Lock line, was sailing that morning for San Francisco. Kelly as usual had his pickings lined up. The mate, a cunning, wiry Scotchman, jumped ashore and looked them over. He lacked one man. There were fifteen of us.

"Are you a sailor?" he asked me.

"Yes, sir," I answered eagerly.

"Have you any discharges?"

"I have one, sir."

"This is from Quebec to Liverpool. It doesn't prove that you are a sailor."

My heart sank. Nevertheless, he finally chose me, probably because I was the youngest and would be the easiest to train. Kelly waved me good-bye. He had two months of my wages in advance, and I had three shillings.

We warped the ship out of the dock. Then the tug-boat took us down the Mersey, and we were out and away to sea on one of the longest voyages I ever made. The ship was three-masted and square-rigged, with a steel hull. She carried twenty-two men before the mast—the carpenter, sailmaker, three mates, a darkey steward, and an English cook.

She was a real lime juicer. Everything we had to eat was weighed out, and our water was measured. The captain was fat and religious. He played on a small organ in his cabin and sang hymns most of the time. The crew represented practically every nationality on the earth.

I learned to fight on board that ship, for there were some tough men in the forecastle—a Dago, whose chief desire when mad was to throw a knife at you, a whale of a Hollander who thought he could whip anyone, a Dane who claimed that he had made John L. Sullivan take water. I must not forget the Greek, who believed in being forearmed, and carried a sharp-pointed marline-spike slung around his neck.

After the tug-boat and pilot had left us it began to blow. It was fair wind out of the English Channel. Although under upper topsails, she soon cleared the land, and ripped away south'ard into fine weather, where I drew my first breath of the trade winds. If there is one place in the world for Romance, it is under tropical skies in a sailing ship. There the sailor builds his castles, and echoes from the past mingle with his thoughts of some pretty girl in a far-away port. Sailors get sentimental when the trade winds blow. They are more cleanly in their habits, too, than in the northern and southern latitudes. It is in the night watches, when the moon shines full, and balmy winds fan the sails, that they spin their best yarns of shipwrecks, and sweethearts, and hard-shelled mates. They are Neptune's children, as harmless as their boasts, and as flighty as the flying-fish that skim the dark waters.

The Channel winds blew us into the north-east

trades; then with every sail set that could catch the breeze we sailed on south, and away for Cape Horn. The sea biscuits weren't bad, but we always looked forward to Thursday and Sunday, when we had a pound loaf of flour bread. The salt horse and lime juice were sparingly served, but we were all forced to drink the juice to avoid getting scurvy.

The big Hollander bossed the forecastle. I longed for Liverpool Jack to trim him, and often I wondered whether I should ever see my friend again. I had been away from home now six months, and in that time I had learned more about human nature than I could have had I lived twenty years in Ireland. I felt responsibility, and had confidence in what I knew about a ship; but I had much yet to learn about the waves and the winds, and the minds of deep-water sailors.

One night as we were nearing the Equator, the middle watch from twelve to two was my wheel. The Dutchman claimed that I had eaten one of his sea biscuits before going to relieve the helmsman. This particular piece of hardtack he was saving to make cracker hash on the following morning. I stoutly denied it, and just to show his brutal authority, he knocked me down with a swing of his powerful fist. I got up, hurt and revengeful. On my way aft to the wheel the third mate noticed the blood dripping from my mouth, and wanted to know who had caused it.

"I don't like that brute," he whispered, "and I'll show you how you can whip him. I'll train you, and by the time we're off Cape Horn you'll be ready."

I hurried off to the wheel, happy in the thought that I had found another champion. The third mate had boxing gloves, which he knew how to handle. He taught me how to box, how to swing for the Dutchman with a knock-out, as well as uppercuts, right and left hooks, and a powerful swing from the hip, which he thought necessary to bring the Dutchman to the deck.

In the meantime the Dane and the Dutchman came together. That was one Sunday afternoon when we were sailing south of the Equator. The fight started over the Dane's washing his clothes in the Dutchman's whack of fresh water. Fresh water was a luxury to drink, let alone the washing of dirty clothes in it. The fat and religious captain was as usual singing his Sunday hymns, the sailors were lying about the deck, and the south-east trades were cooing in the rigging. The gentle roll of the ship was ideal for the occasion. I was particularly interested in this fight, and was hoping that the Dane would give the Dutchman the licking of his life. The Dutchman, for some reason, perhaps because he had injured me, hated me, and made my life in the forecastle as miserable as he could.

They stripped to the waist. Hairy creatures they were, more like animals than men. They fought like two massive bears, hugging and trying to squeeze the life out of each other. They knew nothing about boxing or real fighting. I could see, as the fight went on, that the Dane was beginning to show yellow. He missed a few of his awkward swings, then fell to the deck, exhausted. The Hollander came out victorious, but neither was hurt very badly. The third mate was not supposed to see the fight—his duty should have been to stop it—but he managed to be near and took it all in, carefully noting, for my future benefit, the Dutchman's weaknesses, and assuring me that when I had learned the pivot wallop I should be able to conquer my enemy. This was good news indeed, and I set about my further training with zest.

CHAPTER TWELVE

THE FIGHT OFF CAPE HORN

THE captain had a dozen hens on board for his own private use. Occasionally one would lay an egg. These were royal eggs and could be eaten by the master only. To find an egg when one cleaned the coop was to bring cheer to the commander's heart. The weather was cold now and the hens were timid about laying eggs. Here is where my story of the fight with the Dutchman begins.

We were to the south'ard and west'ard of the Falkland Islands, and almost in the latitude of Cape Horn, but far from being around it. It was then the beginning of summer. The days were long, the winds were becoming threatening and cold. The sea looked boisterous and defiant, with a long, deep, rolling swell from the south-west.

One morning the bosun ordered me to clean out the hen-coop, and to gather in the eggs, should there be any. The captain, complaining about the scarcity of the eggs, said he wondered if someone had been stealing them.

The chicken-coop was in a spare room in the midship's house. While I was scrubbing in there, the big Dutchman stuck his head into the door and shouted:

THE FIGHT OFF CAPE HORN

"You're the damned thief that's been stealing the eggs!"

The mate heard him and came running to the chicken-coop. The captain was walking the poop, and seeing his first mate take on more speed than usual, and wondering what all the noise around the chicken-coop might be, he hurried off the poop and joined the mate.

"There's the man that's been stealing the eggs!" cried the Dutchman. "I saw him just now sucking one."

The mate raved and swore, and the captain took it very much to heart. How dare anyone eat his hens' eggs?

I pleaded, declaring that the Hollander was a liar and a cur, and that I didn't steal the eggs. The Dutchman foamed with rage and said he'd beat me to jelly.

The captain believed the Dutchman, and as punishment, he fined me one month's pay. I cleaned the coop, while the captain and mate walked off. I could hear the captain say: "I knew those hens were laying all the time." I, who knew more about hens than I did about the Lord's Prayer, was well aware of the effect of cold weather upon laying hens, and hoped that the captain would find out some time that hens either cannot or will not lay eggs in iceberg weather.

The Dutchman was waiting for me around the fore part of the forecastle.

"Now," said he, "I'm going to give you a whipping that you will never forget."

In spite of the third mate's instructions not to lose my temper, in view of my recent trouble I found it hard to remain cool. I faced him, grinning with rage, and said: "Come on, you Dutch hound! It's you who will get the whipping."

He rushed for me as if he would swallow me up. I side-stepped and caught him on the eye. My greatest difficulty was in keeping him from getting a hold on me. Back he came at me like an uncaged lion, with his fists flying in front of him. The crew gathered around approvingly, to see a boy not yet nineteen holding his own with a man so much more experienced, and at least fifty pounds heavier.

I caught him again, this time on the mouth, knocking a tooth out and injuring my hand, which had a sickening effect on me. But I had him groggy, and all that was needed was to give him a swing from my hip to bring him to the deck. He rushed me, like all cowards, with his head down, and his black eyes closed. I heard a voice, the third mate's:

"Put it to him now."

I upper-cut him first, then when he lifted his head swung for him. The big lying Dutchman lay crumpled on the deck.

"Now you can take care of yourself on any ship," said the third mate as he bandaged up my hand. I have done it, on more than one occasion.

The Dutchman made many threats as to what he

would do to me some dark night, but I had him cowed, and he knew it. I was respected in the forecastle now, and could grab the first chunk of salt horse and get away with it.

About a week later we struck a Cape Horn blizzard, and while I had thought it blew hard off the Newfoundland Banks, that was a mild storm compared to this one. Gale, hail, snow and sleet we had. Hours we spent reefing the icy topsail, clumsy in our clothes, and cold, and sure that if our stiffened fingers slipped there was a quick, icy grave awaiting us. The seas looked larger to me than the mountains of Ireland. The ship had no buoyancy; her cargo was Scotch whisky, ale and porter, and it lay heavy in her bowels. Seas flooded her fore and aft, and life-lines were rigged on the deck for the crew to work ship.

It was difficult to get any response from the cook these days. He refused to bake our cracker hash, which any cook should do, since it represents to a sailor the final good derived from faithful saving of crumbs. The bean-soup was beyond assimilation, and only a sailor with a shark's stomach could digest it. There was hardly a spot on the cook's face that was not covered with red blotches.

The god of the sea chooses well for the sailor. The cook was removed from the ship the following day.

It was Sunday, and five o'clock in the morning. The gale had not abated, nor had the sea decreased in mountain volume. Storm trysails and lower topsails were the sails she carried. The wind and waves were a point abaft the starboard beam. The seas had a raking sweep at the decks fore and aft the ship. The cook's galley acted as a sea wall for the Cape Horn combers.

Two bells, five o'clock, rang the man at the forecastle head, and as the rolling tones died away in the crisp morning air, we shipped a sea, a rolling, green, white-capped comber; when the decks were clear again we missed the cook, the galley, and the captain's hens. That was the end of the red-spotted cook.

Six long weeks we fought the weather off Cape Horn. Hungry and cold we struggled with the ship, never giving an inch. Icebergs and gales we met and fought. Our clothes were frozen to our backs before it was over, and when the wind at last blew fair for the Pacific Ocean I realized the truth of the sailors' saying, that Cape Horn is the place where Iron Seamen are made.

The Horn is now only for those who seek it without fear. The Panama Canal—the silent canal, as it is called, and no one who does not know the Horn at its worst can appreciate the vast quiet of that term —carries them now. There is no cursing on the ships as the canal takes them, no splicing of the main brace to stave off the fear of death, no chewing of tobacco crumbs to cheat the empty stomachs until the elements would release their death-clutch on the galley stove. Oh, the men that needn't have gone! The rough, simple, brave, abandoned men!

THE FIGHT OFF CAPE HORN

Yet as the years drift by, I can see that a Cape Horn training for our sailors to-day, even for our business and society men, might make better men of the men, and make men of the "sissies," and perhaps help to perpetuate the strength of the human race.

CHAPTER THIRTEEN

HOBOES

SAILORS are simple, light-hearted souls, whose load of yesterday is airy as thistle-down to-day. With a favouring breeze we set all sail, and the sailors chatted and laughed like children. We sang chanties as the yards went up, and our sufferings vanished with the cold. Soon we should be in the tropics again, and then hurrah for the Golden Gate and Sacramento River!

We missed the cook very little and his cooking less. He would have died before we made port. We rigged up a temporary galley and found an old sailor who could make pea-soup. The darkey steward could make bread; anyone could boil salt horse.

The captain grieved over his hens, but still continued singing his favourite hymn:

"Come to thy Father, O wanderer, come!
Someone is praying for you.
Turn from the sin path no longer to roam;
Someone is praying for you."

As we sailed northward into clearer skies, the balmy winds from the South Sea Isles wafted dreams of stars and moon, and other worlds. So the days

HOBOES

passed, through glittering stars, cooing winds, and Capricorn sunsets. After four months and twenty-six days we dropped anchor off Goat Island in San Francisco Bay. I was a man and a sailor now, but keen for new adventures in a country that offered every opportunity.

While we were lying at anchor, even before the ship went to the wharf to unload, a couple of crimps came on board, unhindered because of some ancient custom, and persuaded many of the crew to leave, offering them higher wages if they would sail aboard American ships. We had signed articles in England for the round trip, and any money given a sailor to take ashore was optional with the captain. If the sailor was dissatisfied and left the ship at that port, he sacrificed his pay for the entire voyage.

I refused to go with any of the crimps, but stayed by the ship until she docked, which pleased the third mate very much. He had taught me all he knew about navigation, and was proud of my battling qualities as well. (By the way, the Dutchman had left the ship with the first of the boarding-house crimps.)

When the ship docked, I went aft to the captain and asked him for some money to spend. He grudgingly gave me fifty cents, told me not to spend it all in one night, and promised me another fifty cents the following Saturday. After five months in a lime-juice ship, fifty cents to spend ashore in one week! Steam beer was selling at two mugs for five cents on Pacific Street, and whisky five cents a drink on the Barbary coast. That may sound wonderful indeed to prohibitionized ears, but the stuff was almost as dangerous then as it would be now at that price.

The captain's injustice so hurt me that I left the ship. A crimp soon had me in tow and took me to a sailors' boarding-house. After a few days there I agreed to ship aboard a whaler, to be gone for three years. They pictured to me the beauties of the Arctic Ocean, the icebergs, the musk-ox, the gorgeous Aurora Borealis, and particularly the grand pay I would get from my share in the whale : pay which was supposed to run well up into the thousands by the end of the voyage. The same old story has lured good men into an industry where greed makes fortunes for a few, and keeps thousands of men cheerless and overworked for years, only to release them penniless at the end. I was ignorant, or I should never have signed on.

My bag was already aboard the whaler when someone behind me spoke : "Get your bag and come back on the wharf."

Somewhere I had heard that voice before.

"Come on now, get aboard that ship ; none of your lally-gagging," cried the crimp, fearing for his money.

I turned around in answer to the voice. It was Liverpool Jack. In all my seventeen years on and off the sea, he was the only sailor I ever met who knew how to trim a crimp. I dropped my bag and ran to him, shaking him warmly by the hand.

"Get aboard that ship!" roared the crimp.

"Put your bag in the forecastle," whispered Jack, "then get back on to the wharf."

I was so happy to see him that I ignored his instructions; the result was that I was knocked down, and thrown aboard the whaler.

"There, damn you," bellowed the crimp, "stay there now!"

I picked myself up, and jumped back on to the wharf, full of fight. Three of the boarding-house thugs rushed at me. The first I knocked down; the other two grabbed me, and were in the act of pitching me over the rail on to the hard deck when Liverpool Jack ran to my rescue. Oh, how he could fight! He knocked them right and left, and I being free now, the three crimps were no match for us. We fought, and fought hard on that slippery wharf. The crimps would not hesitate to kill. They had police protection, and a sailor's life in San Francisco wasn't worth much in those days.

They shouted to the mates aboard the whaler for help. Two burly men jumped on to the bulwark rail, but before they landed on the wharf I hit one and Jack the other, and they fell on board. A crowd of longshoremen and sailors were gathering round. The crimps were groggy and had no endurance for further fight. Jack shouted:

"Let's run for it before it's too late!"

He headed up the wharf on a dead run, I after him; we were soon lost in the crowded street, but dangerously near the water-front. "We'll have to get out of the city," panted Jack. "Our lives are not safe now."

We boarded a Mission Street car and rode well out into the country to the end of the line. There we hunted up a quiet place and yarned until the sun set and the misty dampness of 'Frisco Bay sent a chill through us. Then we got up and walked on into the night.

It was fifty miles from San Francisco to San José. Our course along the country road pointed to that city. The winter weather was snappy and a white frost made its appearance on the house-tops and glittered like fool's gold in the rays of the half-moon.

As we plodded on we talked of our experiences since we had separated at Chicoutimi. Jack reached Montreal a few days after he had left me, and finding shipping quiet there, beat it down to Quebec, and shipped on a vessel bound for Valparaiso. As usual he didn't like the ship and left her there. After living in Valparaiso for a month or more doing odd jobs at longshoring, he found a barque bound for San Francisco, and there he had been for seven weeks before we met. Many opportunities there were to ship aboard a whaler, but Jack had a horror of whalers. I think that sometime in his younger life he had probably been shanghaied on one of them.

We were in a country now which I had been told was God's country, where nature abounded in everything for the needy, and wages were high. Little I dreamed, as I walked along that night, that I was living in the panic of 1893, and that hunger's skeleton grinned at me as I passed the milestones. Wages of fifteen dollars a month were not for such men as I that year, when even sturdy, steady, domestic labourers found it hard to get work.

Jack and I, heedless of the currents and reefs we were steering into, hiked on, and at two o'clock in the morning walked into Redwood City, tired and hungry. The town was small in those days. A few lights glimmered through the trees. A dog or two barked at our approach and steeled the night watchman into action. To be sure he was well armed, having his night stick, and a gun strapped to his side. He headed straight for us, his club in his hand.

"Where are you hoboes going?" he shouted.

"We're bound for San Diego," answered Jack.

"Well, keep a-moving," he said. "You ain't a-going to find San Diego in these parts."

We walked along a little farther, when Jack suddenly stopped short. "Listen," he whispered. Then I could hear the chug-chug of a locomotive down in the freight yard.

"Come on," said he, "we'll walk no more. We'll ride in a freight car to San Diego."

I believe that Jack knew that San Diego was in California, but in what part of California I am sure he did not know. I myself am not good at directions except at sea, and in its nearest parallel, the desert, and I have often noticed how free and easy other sailors are with distance on the land. Jack knew, however, that wherever San Diego might be, it was a seaport, and assured me with happy confidence that only the best ships left from there!

An old night watchman in the freight yards told us that a freight was leaving for Fresno shortly, and that there were many empty box cars in it. We crawled into one and hid away in a dark, smelly corner, and were off—unfared passengers cold, and hungry.

We must have slept for a long time, when the door opened, letting in the sun and an unwelcome brakeman.

"Where in hell are you 'boes going?" he roared.

"San Diego," answered Jack, rubbing his eyes.

"Have you any money?"

"Not a damned cent."

"Well, get off the train before I throw you off."

"I have a dollar," said I, but Jack shook my shoulder, and announced his intention of getting off, saying airily that he needed to stretch his legs, anyway. As we alighted among the vineyards, for we had travelled far on that freight train, the brakeman hurled an oath after us, because we, and not he, still had our last dollar.

There was a little town among the vineyards, a cosy little town, with its church and blacksmith shop, looking all new and shiny in the sun, and, still better for us, a Chinese restaurant. There half the dollar fed us heartily, and turned our outlook upon life into gold also. We were not far from Fresno, we were told, but there was no work to be had. The Democrats, under Cleveland, the local gossips said, had bankrupted the country, and the farmers were facing starvation. The only salvation for the country lay with the Populist Party. What a pity that the very men who needed to hear reasonable discussion were, in the days before the radio, farthest removed from any opportunity to listen to it!

I began to long for the roll of a ship and the spray from the deep. I seemed to be going from bad to worse, with fifty cents in my pocket and gloom ahead. When I suggested going back, even if it involved shipping on a whaler, Jack only laughed. Going without a few meals was nothing to him, and beating his way on trains, I discovered, was actually a source of joy. Ships to him were only a means of conveyance to leave lands where adventure had become monotonous.

We learned that there would be a freight train that afternoon for the south. I left Jack, who never walked for pleasure, to take a country stroll. I walked through the vineyards, and saw white men and Japanese pruning the vines. The work looked agreeable, and I felt that I could do it if only I had a job.

When I got back I saw that Jack had been drinking, although it was hard to tell where he could have secured it. As the train came in, and the brakeman warned us off it unless we had money to give him, Jack, more courageous after drinking than I was sober, shouted to me to "catch the gunnels" of the now passing train. He himself suited the action to the word by swinging under and up to rest on the gunwales—the longitudinal rods that are placed close to the ground under the cars.

While I stood passively by, unable to compass this process sufficiently quickly to follow suit, the train gathered speed. Jack waved his hand to me and was gone : into space for another span of years.

CHAPTER FOURTEEN

BENEFIT OF CLERGY

FEELING now more alone than when Jack had left me in Canada, I turned aimlessly and headed off into the country. Presently I came to a lane, and a farm-house, and a man milking cows, chewing tobacco as he milked. His hairy head was buried in the cow's flank, and his boots were crusted with manure. As I approached him, asking if he was the farmer, a girl called from the back porch:

"Father, mother says that you are to be sure to leave enough milk for the calf."

He grunted: "All right, Ellen." Then looking at me out of the corners of his eyes: "Well, suppose I be the farmer here, what do you want?"

"A job," said I brazenly.

"Young feller, I ain't got work enough for myself to do, let alone hiring a man."

"I must have work," said I desperately. "I'm broke, and I've got to earn some money. I know you have work for me to do as long as you have grapes to prune. I can milk cows too, and I'll work cheap."

He looked me over from my shoes up. While I

wasn't very clean, still I was respectable-looking. He handed me a tin bucket.

"Milk old Muley, there by the gate," he said, and I milked old Muley in a hurry. I stripped her clean, for having been raised on a farm, milking was second nature to me.

"Have you another one?" I asked, eagerly handing him the bucket.

"No," he growled, picking up the buckets and starting for the house, "but stay here till I come back; I may have some work for you to do. I'll talk to Ma."

I waited, and hoped, and prayed for a job.

Then the farmer's voice sounded from the house:

"Come on here, stranger."

His wife, a short, fat woman, but rather neat in her gingham dress, greeted me with, "How did you come to be broke?" I told her the whole thing, as a boy would. It seemed ages since I had been in a home. The girl, about seventeen years old, and good-looking, was listening in the pantry.

Evidently the mother approved of me. At any rate, she was the boss of that farm, as was plain to see. "I can give you a week's work," she said, "but mind you, I can't pay much. Fifty cents a day and board."

"I'll take it," I answered cheerfully.

We had supper together, I leading in the conversation. The food wasn't bad, considering the times. Potatoes and bread and tea there were in plenty, and a slice of fried bacon for each one. Then there were stewed pears for dessert.

The farmer made a bed for me in the barn with the cows and horses, and I went to sleep, but fitfully, for however pleasant the noises and stampings and barkings of farm animals may be to a farm lad, they are very different from the voices of the sea, and the cobwebbed rafters of a barn, loomy and spaceful as they are, release one too suddenly from the oppression of the ship's forecastle ceiling.

At four o'clock he called to me: "Get up and milk the cows."

"Where's the pump?" I inquired, turning out.

"What do you want the pump for, this time of morning?"

"I want to wash my head and face."

"You'll find it on the porch," he mumbled. "I don't wash till breakfast-time."

I doubted if he did then, as he was never either washing or washed when I saw him, and I'm quite sure that he couldn't have combed his hair even if he had tried.

I spent one week working around the barn and stables, cleaning them out. It had been many months since they had been touched by the hand of man. I afterwards found that some farmers prefer to move their barns, rather than cart the manure away. Then they buy fertilizer for the land.

The girl and I became fast friends, which I could

see did not please the mother, who grew colder towards me at meals.

"Can you prune grapes?" asked the farmer one evening, after I had earned three dollars in the Land of the Golden Gate.

"Oh, yes," said I, "I can do anything."

This utterance proved my downfall. I had never pruned grape-vines, but I had seen the Japs and others do it, and it seemed to me that all that was necessary was to clip off the long trailing vines.

Next morning he gave me the pruning shears, and with a wave of the hand started me on the thirty or more acres he had to prune. I began with a will, hoping to show my appreciation of his giving me work, and slashed right and left, pruning close to the vines without regard for bud or balance. Towards noon my master came to see how I was doing, and to my dismay, swore he'd have me shot. So violent was his rage and the anguish of his wife, who mourned the day she had ever befriended me, that I was grateful for the three dollars I had earned and a drink from the pump.

This much better off than I had been a week ago, and with some knowledge of how *not* to prune, I waved my hat to the girl, and started up the main road, reflecting upon my fortune. To this day I laugh when I think of that adventure, and my utter meekness about it. Many years after I was invited to do pruning in the vineyard of a lady who ran her own ranch, and refused to allow me to stay there unless I would work for her. Tempted as I was, I ran no risks.

"Madam," I said, "you can ask me to dig, or carry wheat, or milk your cows, but don't ask me to prune grape-vines."

"You're very particular," said she.

"Yes," said I, "and I have reason to be."

How to get to a seaport was my next problem, for I had made up my mind that the sea was the place for me. I was about as close to San Francisco as I was to San Diego. I walked to the village and sat down on a pile of railroad ties to ponder the past and speculate upon the future. I was beginning to believe that I had made a fatal mistake. I should never have left home. I doubted if in this strange country of barking dogs and selfish people, I could ever make a go of it. I resolved then and there to follow Liverpool Jack to San Diego and from there try to ship for England. A comforting thought, but by no means to be borne out in the event.

Suddenly there was a shout from behind me. Turning quickly, I saw five men coming towards me.

"Where are you going, 'bo?" one of them called.

They were unshaven, dirty and ragged, and their shoes were worn soleless.

"I'm bound for San Diego," said I, glad of their cheerfulness.

"Keep away from there," said the tallest of the men. "We've just come from there. I'm here to tell you it's the hungriest part of the state." Then he told me their story, while the others pulled themselves up to the pile of ties, or stood around commenting. They couldn't find work anywhere, or little of anything to eat. One had a wife and children back east. For the sake of a sick little one he had come west to find a home for them all, and he hadn't the nerve to write how dismally he had failed. Had names meant anything to me then, I should have been interested in that man's name, for it was well known. So it is in the west; I knew a longshoreman who became one of the most influential of United States senators; a woman who took in washing in my day afterwards became prominent in New York upper-class society.

The narrow waists and long cheek-bones of these five men corroborated their statements that they were half starved. I could not sit there with money in my pocket and see men go hungry. I invited them to go with me to the Chinese restaurant, and then and there got the worth of my three dollars, as I saw the smile of appreciation spread over those emaciated faces.

They declined my invitation to the Chinese restaurant as an imposition, but took two of my three dollars to buy food to cook. The tall one ran to the village store. The others found some cooking tins and started a fire. In less than an hour they were eating, and what a meal they had! Potatoes, bread, steak, and coffee. They invited me to eat with them, but I preferred to watch them eat, for I wasn't hungry. My stomach wasn't empty, and my

BENEFIT OF CLERGY

pleasure was in watching them fill theirs—a pleasure that more thrifty people cannot feel, for they have no last dollar.

Their waistbands being now expanded, the talk of my guests became more optimistic. The tall one spoke:

"Do you see that church over there?"

"Yes," I replied.

"Men like ourselves are always sure of a dollar from the priest who lives there. But here's the trouble," and he licked his lips, "you've got to put on the gloves and box with him or you don't get anything. He's mighty handy with the mitts."

"Did you try him out?" I asked with interest.

"Nothing doing. I met a man down the road a piece who said he took the beating of his life for a silver dollar, and he sure looked it."

Towards evening a north-bound freight pulled in and stopped. The five men said good-bye, and as she started to move, like the professionals they were, they grabbed hold of the gunwales and slid under the train as if they were going to bed. They were off, and I was alone again—alone with one silver dollar.

I thought of the priest and the possibility of getting another dollar. I could make good use of one. I walked over to the church, and there, sitting on the steps, was the priest. He could see, I suppose, what I was after, for he jumped to his feet, stretched, and felt his muscles. For a moment I hesitated. The size of him sent a shudder through me. Somewhere, from out of childhood's memory chest, rose the spectre of THE OGRE who strangled unwary wayfarers.

I wished him a polite "good evening," and he asked me what I wanted.

"I want to earn a dollar."

"Come right in here, my boy," and he led me into a small house that adjoined the church.

In a room that was not much larger than eight by ten he stopped. I pulled off my coat without a word, while he ostentatiously juggled some dumb-bells.

Then: "Are you sure that you want to tackle me?" he inquired.

I should have liked to say no, but I wanted his dollar so badly that it was worth a beating to me. I assured him that I was ready.

He handed me the gloves, and put his on without further comment or question. We squared away. He caught me a wallop on the ear, and I went down. When I got up on my feet again I forgot all about the dollar I was earning and the man who wore the broadcloth. I felt that I was back on a ship, and I wasn't going to lose a fight.

I caught him on the jaw and staggered him, following it with an upper-cut that knocked him down. When he got up he was bleeding freely, and science lost its art. He started slugging. Here was where I shone. I whipped him and whipped him well, until he cried enough.

As if nothing had happened, he took me to the

sink, where I washed my blood and his blood off of me. Then he wished me good-bye and God-speed, with apostolic dignity, and my reward was not one dollar—but FIVE!

CHAPTER FIFTEEN

HOGGING IT

It was dark now and the air cold. I crawled into an empty box car that stood on a side track. I must have slept, for I awoke with a start as another car struck the one in which I was. Then the whole thing started to move. I was off on a train, and I didn't know where. Through the night I looked out of a side door, but couldn't tell whether we were headed north or south. No one bothered about me. I doubt if the brakeman knew I was there. It was noon the next day when I crawled out of the car. I discovered that I was headed north, and guessed that I was near Sacramento, and about seven hundred miles north of San Diego, which proved to be true.

"Well," thought I, "I'll have to make the best of it. I'm ninety miles from San Francisco, and that's some satisfaction." Jack's horror of whaling ships and his cursing of them and all that belonged to them came back to me now with force, and the thought of the slithery crimps made me wish I was anywhere else.

But hunger often rules our destinies, and I was hungry. The train had stopped at a siding, and there was no town in sight. I walked off and followed a country road; there I saw a man ahead of me driving a sorrel horse hitched to a wagon with milk-cans in the back. I overtook him and spoke to him, asking him if he knew of any chance to work in the neighbourhood.

He pulled up the reins, and shouted in a clear Irish brogue:

"Whoa there, Jerry!"

"Can ye milk cows?" he asked, looking down on me, and there was something about him that took me back to Ireland.

"Yes, I can," I answered.

"Jump up on the wagon, then," he commanded. "The job I'll be giving ye won't be much," he went on, "but if ye're broke ye ought to be glad of anything."

He jerked the reins, gave Jerry a cut with the whip, and we were off to O'Donnell's farm, this being the land of my new master. He was past sixty, white-haired and wrinkled, his hands showing the toil of years, his upper lip long, broad, and sadly humorous. It lifted frequently to show a mouth almost destitute of teeth.

We pulled up at his farm, if a farm you would call it. A small barn and the house where he lived comprised the buildings of the place. Ten acres of land was the farm, and a few hungry cows the visible stock. We unhitched Jerry, putting him away in a dirty stall, with a forkful of hay for his dinner.

Then I went into the shack where O'Donnell had preceded me and was cooking. It was a large, bare, dirty room, without partitions. On the table was a boiled bullock's heart, cooked not too recently, which he was carving. "A foine meal for a healthy man," he said. Boiled heart, bread, and skimmed milk we had. He informed me that he always said grace before meals, and proceeded to do so. Although there was not much on the table to be grateful for, I echoed his " amen " loudly and thankfully. I was hungry, and the bread and heart disappeared like snow before a summer sun.

"Now," said O'Donnell, wiping his mouth on the oilcloth cover, " I'll tell ye what I'll be wanting ye to be doing. There's fifteen cows to milk, and I'll be helping ye some. Ye get up in the morning about three o'clock, and start to milk. By four o'clock we'll have it in the cans; then I drive to town and deliver it to me customers. I'm back here by nine o'clock. The reason that I'm late to-day is that I've been dickering with a man about buying hogs."

"Oh, you're going into the hog business ? " said I, pushing back from the table.

"Yes, I'm thinking about it. There's money in hogs these days, and I have a foine place for them. But to get back to yere work. As I said, I get home about nine o'clock. While I'm gone ye'll do the chores, clean out the cow barn, and turn the cows out to pasture. It isn't much grass that's in the field, but shure and they get the exercise.

HOGGING IT

"Now, me boy," he concluded, getting up from the table, "after ye've finished, water the little roan horse; he's in the stall in the north end of the barn. I'll be home by the toime ye have the work done."

I was just congratulating myself that I was not asked to do what I didn't know how, when he turned around, saying:

"Hold on, me boy. Do ye know how to drive a team?"

This was no time for unmanly weakness. I gulped hard and assured him that I did; but it was not the fact. However, I found afterwards that I could do it very well. He went on to tell me that he had bought a lot of hop-poles from a man who had a yard down by the Sacramento River, and that he was hauling them to sell to a Chinese laundry. This would be part of my work, and I would be paid twenty dollars a month for it.

I felt that I had found a friend here in this strange old man. He told me a great deal about his affairs, and rather hinted that I go into partnership with him in the hog business. It seemed that there was money in the dirty creatures. Anyway, it would be a start in this new country, and I wrote home and told my mother how well I was getting along, and how prosperous I should be some day, thinking how delighted she would be over my fine prospects, quite regardless of present aspects.

We did become partners in the hog business, and in the three months that I worked for O'Donnell my wages went with his money to increase the stock over the sixty hogs we already had; and as things looked brighter I even neglected my clothes to save money. I wasn't presentable, but that didn't matter, for wasn't I going to make a lot of money right away? Then, I thought, I should branch out for myself on a large scale.

My work these days seemed never to be done, what with milking, feeding the stock, hauling wood to the Chinese laundry, and in the evening taking O'Donnell into the small neighbouring towns where he made impassioned stump speeches for the Populist Party.

He was very particular about his speeches, and Sundays were devoted to rehearsing them in the barn, the acoustics in the shack being considered inadequate. At least in the barn we had an appreciative audience, for every other phrase was punctuated by a chorus of moos, brays, whinnies, and cackles.

"I stand here to-night before ye, men," O'Donnell would commence, "a praycher in the cause of the People's Party. From the tops of the mountains to the broad expanse of the Pacific, let me words ring home their message!"

Our luck on these excursions varied. We were always sure of an audience, but not so sure of a flattering one. One night, while O'Donnell was warming up to his subject, someone put a thistle under Jerry's tail, and as we started off he ran away, spilling us both out of the wagon. We had to walk eight miles home. O'Donnell seemed to take the

HOGGING IT

inconvenience philosophically; the cause was just, there had to be martyrs. We might as well be cheerful ones.

Well I remember the last load of hop-poles I hauled to the Chinaman's laundry. I had become acquainted with some of the Portuguese living in the bottom lands of the Sacramento River, along which my road lay. Since it was the last load, Manuel Da Costa insisted that I take a drink with him of home-brewed Portuguese brandy, known in those parts as " jackass brandy."

He had been kind to me, helping me often to free the wagon wheels when they sank too deep into the soft river mud. To please him I took a drink, then another, for it tasted good, and did not seem to have a kick to it. Then bidding him good-bye, I jumped into the wagon and drove off.

There was a freshet in the Sacramento River and it ran foaming. After riding about a mile the jackass brandy took complete possession of me. Quickly and quietly it did its deadly work. Regardless of danger or icy chill, I decided that the river looked good to me, and without a moment's hesitation I climbed down, tied the horse, jumped fully clothed into the mad, roaring river, and swam across it and back again.

The icy water had no effect whatever on me, nor did I feel ashamed of myself until long after I had untied the horse and headed, wet as I was, for the town. I never told O'Donnell, knowing full well his feelings on the subject of temperance. As time went on, and I realized how narrow had been my escape from drowning, I decided that never again would I be tempted to drink jackass brandy.

It was now a little over a year since I had left home, and my three months were drawing to a close, when the time seemed to be right for expansion in the hog business. O'Donnell bought garbage and hauled it every morning from the town to feed the stock. They throve on the feed, in the muddy coolness of the ditch where they buried themselves. We were to kill ten of the heaviest in a few days and sell them. With the money we would buy shoats five weeks old to raise and fatten for the market.

Now we could begin to build castles, for six months more would yield us substantial money. My castle took the form of a cosy little farm, and included a cosy little wife too, for I was becoming much enamoured of a red-haired lassie, whose father raised strawberries. She liked me in spite of my seedy clothes, and the way I had of talking to my pigs; in spite also of her father, who told her that I was nothing but seaweed that the storm blew in.

Nevertheless, I kissed her one day through the fence—a barbed-wire fence at that—and a thrill went through me the like of which I had never known before. I began to long for the complementary companionship of her, and I pictured her sharing my days, and bringing my lunch to me at the plough.

How full of pleasant nothingness were my dreams!

HOGGING IT

They proved but spectres on a wasteless sea—the closer I sailed to them the farther away they faded. Two days after my kiss the hog farm was in mourning. Every last one of the hogs died from hog cholera.

I dug holes for them and covered them up where they lay, and as I buried them I bitterly cursed my luck. What had I done to merit this blow of Fate? Years afterwards, while sailing mate on a ship in the South Seas, I read in a magazine how to guard against hog cholera. Poor old O'Donnell and I knew nothing about vaccinating hogs, and I doubt if more than a few people in the neighbourhood knew about it at that time.

The hogs were buried, and the sun set on Youth and Old Age huddled together in the shack, each complaining after his fashion. We supped together on beef heart and boiled potatoes, and when the candle burned low I blew it out and each went to his own bed, a shakedown of straw on the floor of the shack: O'Donnell to dream, perhaps, of the long ago when life was not a question of potatoes with or without beef heart, and held some hope for the failing years; I to turn towards to-morrow's dawn when I should make a new start—not with hogs this time, but under flapping sails on windy seas, where the squeal from the swivel block would soothe the dirge of lost hopes.

O'Donnell said good-bye to me with some degree of sorrow, and from out of his old soppy overalls fished nine dollars.

"Here, take this," he said. "If I had more I'd gladly give it to ye. Ye're not the bad sort of lad."

I thanked him, and with a heavy heart left him to bid good-bye at the next farm. Walking across a field that I had recently ploughed, it seemed that the new soil had a longing-to-remain smell for me: an odour that took me back home to the springtime of the year, when the ploughing was being done, and the bevelled furrows crumbled under the sun heat of the day. They were crushing memories, and I felt them keenly.

As I squeezed through the barbed-wire fence and into the farm of my sweetheart's father, O'Donnell called after me:

"I say, if ye ever happen around here again I'll be glad to see ye, but wherever ye go don't forget to tell them about the People's Party."

I assured him that I would, whether on land or sea.

Mr. Curran, the girl's father, was hoeing strawberries.

"I hear that your hogs died," he snapped as I approached.

"Yes, every one of them."

"Well, I expected as much. It takes men to raise hogs."

He continued hoeing his strawberries. "What are you going to do now?" he asked presently.

"Oh," said I humbly, "I'm going back to sea."

"I'm thinking that's the place for you."

"I'm going to say good-bye to your daughter Ellen," said I, walking towards the house. He grunted assent like one of my dying sows. Ellen was waiting for me. She knew that I was leaving. Whatever her father had said about me, I knew that it was nothing good, but still she was fond of me.

"Ellen, I have come to say good-bye. I had hopes of being able to stay, but you have heard about the hogs."

"Yes," she said, "I've heard nothing else around this house. Father said you'd sure have to go now."

I kissed her good-bye, and there were tears in the eyes of both of us. We were too young to pledge ourselves to each other, and I never saw her again, but I am sure that Ellen made some lonely man happy.

CHAPTER SIXTEEN

JACKASS BRANDY AGAIN

THE railroad fare from Sacramento to San Francisco was two dollars and fifty cents. I bought a ticket and rode there—to the City of Crimps. I knew what to expect once I fell into their hands, but beggars cannot be choosers; six dollars wouldn't last long, and sooner or later it would be a sailors' boarding-house for me. From there I would be away to the ends of the earth on anything that carried sail.

When I stepped off the train in San Francisco I walked around like a stray dog smelling for the home trail. The lights flickered in the evening shadows; the smell from Fourth Creek, where the city sewage emptied into Mission flats, was thick and nauseating; coastwise schooners were discharging lumber in the creek, and that part of the city was as tough as the Barbary Coast.

At the corner of Fourth and Berry Streets stood a saloon, which was owned by a Dane, whose Irish wife was bartender. It seemed odd to me afterwards that I chose this saloon to go into, and certainly Fate awaited me there, in the person of a man about sixty years old. As I entered he was in the

JACKASS BRANDY AGAIN

act of raising a glass of whisky to his lips, and immediately asked me to join him. I thanked him and ordered a glass of steam beer.

He introduced himself as Captain Glass, now master of a bay scow. He was entering into a discussion of its merits in an absorbing manner, when a man in a Seymour coat tightly buttoned to the chin, and a cap pulled down over his left eye, swaggered into the saloon, deliberately picked up the captain's whisky from the bar, and drank it. The captain made a lunge at him with both fists—and missed him.

Then the crook, as deliberately as he had drunk the whisky, knocked the old captain down on the sawdust floor. As he lay there I could see a little copper button shining in the lapel of his pilot cloth coat. I didn't know then what the button meant, but a few minutes later I learned that it was the insignia of the Grand Army of the Republic, and that the captain had fought in the Civil War.

The Irishwoman dropped my beer, wailing: "Sure and where's the police now? Arra, ye never can find them when ye want them!"

I threw off my coat and cap and flung them on the bar as I flew at the crook. I was so enraged that I forgot the training the third mate on the lime-juicer ship had given me. Twice I was knocked down before I realized that my present style of fighting favoured the crook. Then I collected my wits, got into position, and gave him the whipping of his slimy life. To finish with gusto I picked him up, carried him to the street, and threw him into the gutter. Both my eyes were black, my nose was bleeding, and my lip was cut.

The old captain was on his feet again when I backed into the saloon, and helped me on with my coat. Three teeth were missing from his false set —he didn't know whether he had swallowed them or not—an egg-shaped lump was also developing on his right jaw. Willing as he was to talk, he had difficulty in moving his jaws.

We had our drink in peace this time. He praised me for my good fighting, and the Irishwoman, not to be outdone, said:

" Sure and it's as pretty a piece of fighting as ever I seen in this bar-room. Drink up, me boys, and have another one on me."

" What do you do for a living ? " asked the captain, steadying his jaw with his hand so that he could speak.

" I'm a sailor, looking for a ship."

" I'll give you a job. Two dollars a day with board."

" All right, sir, I'm your man. But what's the work to be ? "

" Sailing with me up the Sacramento River. As I said, I'm the captain of a little schooner, or bay scow as they call them here. I sail up the river and carry cargo back to the city. Now we'll take another drink and go on board."

We went out and down to the Mission wharf, where the captain had a small boat moored to the slip. We stepped into her, and I rowed off under his direction out into the bay, where anchor lights and side lights were as thick as stars in the heavens above. They seemed to be welcoming me home.

I rowed past screeching tugs and warning ferry boats and square-rigged ships with raking masts, that loomed out of the darkness like gigantic creatures of the deep, come out to breathe the night air.

"That's her over there. Pull to your right a little."

I saw the outline of a small two-mast schooner riding gracefully in the ripples of an ebb tide. We boarded her and tied the dinghy astern. The captain invited me into the cabin to have a bite to eat before we set sail. The cabin was small and reminded me of the Swede's sloop in Glasgow. It was clean, and there was a place for everything; the old man had a sense of order.

The small stove that was lashed to the bulkhead smoked as he lit the fire. While he was cooking the supper I went up on deck to look around my new ship. She was about seventy tons, round bottom and centre-board. The lower masts and topmasts had been scraped and a coat of oil rubbed into them. Their pine brightness gave them a lofty appearance against the starry horizon. The main boom looked large for so small a craft; it projected about fifteen feet over the stern. The sails were furled in gaskets and neatly stowed between the gaffs and the booms, the decks were clean, and all ropes coiled neatly in sailor fashion.

"Come on," called the captain with difficulty on account of his aching jaw, "and have something to eat. It's ready now."

We munched in silence, I guarding my cut lip from the hot "Wienies," the captain nibbling at his delicacies with a groan. We washed the food down with hot coffee that to me was delicious in spite of its leathery taste. When the dishes had been put away we went out on deck to set the mainsail, heave up the anchor, and give her the jib and foresail. So we were off with the night breeze to Clarksburg on the Sacramento River, for a cargo of baled hay.

The captain was a thorough sailor and knew every move of his little craft. He pointed out channel lights with one hand while he steered with the other. I could hardly see them, for my eyes were very sore and swollen. I wondered how the crook was feeling by that time, and whether I should ever run across his trail again.

There were stretches in the river where the wind would be fair, and again we would round a bend where it was dead ahead. Here he would haul the little schooner dead on to the wind and beat it to where the breeze was fair again. In this way we made Clarksburg in two days against the current, and sailed right up to the bank, dropping the sails and making her fast to the cottonwood trees, for there was no wharf to tie her to.

The baled hay we were to take aboard was piled high up on the river bank, and loading it was hard

JACKASS BRANDY AGAIN

work for me, since strength was what I used instead of the handy jerk and heave that old hands acquire. So that after working in the hot sun all day, fighting mosquitoes at night, and drinking muddy river water, I was pretty well used up by the time we were loaded. The captain seemed to thrive. He knew the trick of loading, and, old as he was, he could work rings around me.

In three days we had filled the hold and stowed most of the deck cargo, which was the greater part of the whole. To-morrow we should start for San Francisco, and that evening the captain asked me to finish loading while he went for a walk.

About nine o'clock he came back, roaring drunk. He carried a jug which he handed to me.

"Drink some of that, young fellow," he said thickly.

"What is it?" I asked.

"It don't make a damned bit of difference what it is. Drink it, anyway. I'll tell you this much," he growled as he fell over the cabin stool, "it's the world's greatest cure for chills 'n' fever."

What chills and fever were I did not know then, although I was to find out soon enough, nor what the "world's greatest remedy" might be. So I said: "Captain, I'll not touch it till you tell me what it is."

He tumbled into his bunk with a groan. Then he tried to get out of the bunk and couldn't. He muttered softly as his head fell back on the dirty pillow: "Jackass brandy."

Jackass brandy again! None of that for me! I

put the jug away, and, taking a blanket and a piece of mosquito netting, went up on deck to sleep.

At four o'clock in the morning the captain came up with a tin dipper to take a drink out of the river. Seeing me asleep between the tiller ropes, he shouted: "What did you do with that jug?"

In vain I urged him not to drink any more. He would have it, so I finally told him where it was, and he went down to the cabin after it.

I rolled out of the blanket, took off my clothes, and jumped overboard for a refreshing swim. Better than that other time, when I had the kick of the jackass brandy to thank for an icy plunge!

When I came aboard again the captain, apparently quite sober, was elevating the deck platform in line with the load of hay, in order to see where to steer. He told me to make the coffee while he reefed the fore and mainsail, which was necessary with so high a deckload.

The captain drank my coffee, but refused to eat anything, saying his stomach was out of order, which was not, I thought, to be wondered at. At nine o'clock that morning we let go from the cottonwoods, set the sails, and drifted away with the current.

CHAPTER SEVENTEEN

CONSEQUENCES

THE wind was light until we came to where the river grew wider. There the breeze and current favoured us. The captain refused to let me steer, thinking I knew very little about that kind of sailoring. Seeing the jug of brandy beside him on the platform, I felt reasonably alarmed, with the whole day before us and the captain drinking from nine o'clock in the morning.

So the day passed, without many words spoken between us. He insisted on standing at the wheel, hovering over the jug that went to his lips too often. I pleaded with him, but got no response. There were moments when I'd stand beside him cursing inwardly and biting back the fears that came crowding to my mind. But his power to steer seemed independent of his condition, which amazed me. Since then I have lived to see many men like that, and I now believe that they were governed by some guiding power outside the conscious mind.

At about eleven o'clock that night the breeze grew strong, and as we rounded the curve in the river where the wind changed, the booms flew over on the other tack with a lightning bang. I had to shout to the captain to duck his head, which he did automatically. If the main boom should catch him—well, I hated to think what would happen.

"All right, young fellow," he stuttered as he dodged the boom. "I'm a' right. Fashtes trip ever made. Some fash schooner——"

While he took another drink the schooner lay over till the baled hay on the lee side dragged in the water.

I went down into the cabin to make coffee. I thought it might neutralize the brandy and sober him up a bit. Even before I had the fire going I heard the booms swing over, and a deep thud in the cockpit. My heart almost stopped beating. I felt as if I were paralysed.

There was no doubt in my mind as to what had happened. I knew that everything was waiting for me there above: the schooner in danger of being beached, and the captain at least badly hurt. Urged by necessity for action, I jumped to the deck like a man with years of wisdom behind him. I was in possession of faculties I had never known before—and that since have never forsaken me in emergencies.

I ran to where I thought the captain lay. He was there, with blood oozing from his ears and nose, stricken down at last by the mighty swing of the main boom. The wind was whistling through the rigging. The schooner was only two hundred feet from the river bank.

Jumping for the wheel platform and climbing it, I

clutched the wheel, putting it hard down and bringing the schooner up into the wind, heading upstream. Then by dropping the peak of the mainsail and hauling the jib well to windward, I put her out of sailing commission. She would drift with the current down the middle of the river without danger to herself. That done, I ran aft again to the captain.

When I had carried him down into the cabin, I could see by the light of the candle that he was still breathing. How badly he was hurt I could not see. He could not answer when I asked.

Gently I lifted him into the bunk, and in straightening out his legs I discovered that the left one was broken below the knee. His face was covered with blood, and there was a deep scalp wound at the back of his head. His eyes were partly open, the pupils turned upwards, and the lips a pale blue.

I made him as comfortable as I knew how, bandaged his head, and washed the blood away, while I tried to think what I should do. If he died, I might be held to blame. I knew nothing of his affairs, nor even who was the owner of the schooner. What if she should be wrecked? The captain, the vessel, and the river were all strangers to me, and I was alone with these irresponsible forces.

The flapping of the main peak stirred me to action. I jumped to the deck and surveyed the vessel and the night. I could barely trace the outline of the river banks, but beyond them I knew lay uninhabited tule lands. If there was a doctor this side of San Francisco I did not know it, nor at the moment did I seem to know much of anything at all, since my initiative of a few minutes ago had now given place to a mind as variable as the weather-vane upon my father's barn. I actually took time to wish I were at home and asleep in the Irish linen sheets, to awake in the morning and find this only a dream.

The wind now increased, and drops of rain fell. The fresh-water waves lapped with uncanny sound along the sides of the schooner; so different it was from the wash of the great salt ocean. I turned and ran back to the cabin, to the semblance of human companionship.

This time the captain showed signs of consciousness. His eyes were wide open and he groaned as if in great pain. He might live, I thought, and a new hope sprang up in me. I would try to sail the schooner to 'Frisco Bay. It was a daring thing to attempt, but——

I poured some of the muddy river water into the captain's mouth. It gurgled down his throat, and noised as though it rippled over a shallow fall.

"How are you now, sir?"

He looked up at me and said, in a sort of strangling whisper:

"Look out for the schooner. Don't bother about me."

"Shall I take her in?"

He didn't answer, but his head waved a feeble assent. The candle in the bottle candlestick had burned low, the dripping wax had formed a tape-like ribbon down the side of the bottle. I blew the light out and jumped to the deck, set the main peak, ran forward and slacked over the main jib, and back again to the wheel, when she filled away and gathered speed. I put her about and pointed her down the river.

The wind was strong now, but it favoured me, and we were off with God for a pilot, and in me the instinct of a sailor.

It seemed ages till daylight. We had no time, and the old nickel-plated watch was in the captain's pocket. I wondered if he was dead, but could not leave the wheel to find out. Gusts of wind came at times so powerfully it was with difficulty that I kept the schooner from turning over. When this happened I had to luff so close to the river bank that there was danger of running into it.

In the loneliness and darkness I began to pray, and I prayed that night as I have never prayed before or since. I knew the prayers my mother had taught me then. I can't say that I use them of late years, for I have developed a kind of prayer of my own.

Wet from the rain and shivering with cold, I stood at the wheel and watched the antics of the wind and the schooner, until with the first faint streaks of dawn I saw outlined against a hazy hill the bulky form of San Quentin State Prison. I recognized it because the captain had pointed it out to me on our way up the river.

It was a beacon of hope to me. Across the bay,

ten or twelve miles away, lay Mission Flats. There was plenty of sea-room now. I was tempted to let go of the wheel and take a look at the captain, but feared that if I should find him dead I would be too much alarmed to keep command of the schooner. Nor could I help him much if he were alive; so I concluded to make the best time I could to port.

About ten o'clock that Monday morning I lowered the sails and dropped anchor at Mission Flats, and hesitatingly entered the cabin, fearing the worst. But there was yet some life in him. He was breathing hard, with a hollow rattling sound in his throat.

I left him and pulled ashore in the little boat that had been towing astern all night. At the Dane's saloon in Berry Street, which occurred to me as the nearest place to go for help, I found Kitty behind the bar. I told her what had happened and that I wanted someone who could help me get the captain to the hospital at once. She put her hands on her fat hips, and looking out of the window remarked:

"Sure and I knew that something would happen to poor auld Captain Glass."

Then she spun into action. "Hans, you dirty loafer, come here," she cried. "There's work for ye to do."

Her husband appeared as if by magic. A short, thick-set man he was, coatless, and wearing green elastic silk bands with pink bows around his sleeves. He called an ambulance and a policeman, and I rowed him and the doctor to the schooner, where we found the captain still alive. We moved him to the boat, but he died before we reached the wharf.

The jug, by the way, I took ashore with me, and fortunately too, for I had much to explain to the police; so for the first time that jug proved to be my friend.

The agent for the schooner, to whose office I presently found my way, listened to my story without emotion or comment. When I had finished he merely nodded and said quite casually:

"Well, do you think you can run her?"

"Yes, sir," and my voice broke with eagerness, "I think I can."

"All right, then, unload the hay up the bay" (I forget the name of the place he told me), "and from there go up to Porta Costa and get a load of salt."

That was the last of Captain Glass. Unwept and unsung, he passed as many a worthier man has done, and his little bronze button went with him into the humble grave, whose whereabouts I do not even know.

I felt proud of my new position. This was sure and good money, upwards of four hundred dollars a month. Being not yet twenty years old, and the year one of panic and scarcity of work, I thought that it was the sea for a sailor and hogs for the land-lubber.

So I went about my business, hiring a man to help me, and running the schooner without mischance for four months. Then fortune, perhaps fearing that she was spoiling me, deserted me entirely. I contracted malarial fever. Nothing that I could do was of any help, and with the patent medicines I bought, and the whisky and quinine, the doctor's bills I had to pay, and my despair at growing continually weaker, it began to look as if I was to leave the venture in worse condition than I was when I fought for the captain in the saloon on Berry Street.

I left the schooner after four months, when it became apparent that I must do so in order to live. When I left her I had twelve hundred dollars in my pocket. After two months ashore the amount had dwindled sadly. I kept writing home how well I was doing, for my mother's joy at my good fortune was not to be lightly destroyed. Her letters were my only consolation in those trying weeks. Little did she know what I was to pay for having been the captain of a San Francisco bay schooner.

Chills and fever usually hit me in the forenoons, and would last for about three hours on alternate days. Between times I was limp, dizzy and listless, longing to be quit of life.

CHAPTER EIGHTEEN

THE CARPENTER'S CLUTCH

I WISH that I could have grasped then the knowledge that came to me years afterwards of a power working through my subconscious self to safeguard my conscious self from calamity. It seems well, while looking backward, to narrate certain happenings here that have proved of vital import to the course of my life.

I was on Vancouver Island in the little coal-mining town of Ladysmith. Chainless bicycles were new to me then. Nevertheless I rode one down a steep hill. I had been told to back-pedal in order to put the brake on, if I found myself going too fast. So down I coasted, relying on the brake. At the bottom of the hill there was a sharp turn to the left over a steel bridge. I tried to back-pedal, but the brake would not work. Fear took possession of me, and choosing what seemed only a slender chance, I ran the bicycle into the rocky hanging wall of the hill. The result was a smash-up, of course. My shoulder was terribly bruised, but otherwise I was all right.

All that night I walked my room in the most excruciating pain. By daylight I was out in the street seeking relief in the cold air. My shoulder had turned black down to the elbow. To move was torture. "I must see a doctor at once," I thought, as I walked through the town's main street. The first person I met that early morning was a man who could see I was in some trouble.

"Hello!" said he, "what's up with you?"

I told him.

"That's nothing," said he.

I looked at him peevishly, sorry that I had spoken. But he went on:

"Do you see that house up there, with the little green fence around it?"

Yes, certainly I could see it.

"Well, go up there and see Smith the carpenter. He'll take care of you. Hurry now, he's building a house in the country, and he goes away early."

"I don't want a carpenter. It's a doctor I'm looking for," I replied, disgusted by his lack of comprehension.

He pointed a reproving finger at me, but without further explanation repeated:

"Get up to that house. Smith'll cure you."

With that he turned and walked away, while I stood silent, listening to the crunching of the pebbles under his hob-nailed boots.

"Any port in storm," said I to myself. So I headed for Smith's.

He was up and cooking his breakfast. I told him what had happened.

"Wait till I swallow my coffee," he said, "and I'll be with you."

As I looked at him I felt badly discouraged, while the pain in my shoulder seemed to grow worse. A little man he was, with fuzzy beard and head. His hands were short, thick and calloused. "How can a creature like that help me?" I thought. "What I need is the skilled hand of a doctor to set my shoulder and then paint it with arnica." Meanwhile the little man sat drinking his coffee with calm composure and seemingly not at all conscious of my presence. When he had finished, he wiped his beard with the fullness of his hand.

"Come upstairs to the parlour," he said. I dogged up behind him, sceptical.

"Take that chair and sit down," he ordered. Yet his voice was soft and there was a gentleness about him that I had not noticed downstairs. He drew a chair and sat down in front of me.

"You think you have pain in that shoulder," he said, touching it.

I squirmed away. "Could the man be crazy?" I thought.

"Shoot your arm right up over your head," he said.

I ground my teeth and laughed with pain.

"A team of horses couldn't move it," I managed to reply.

"Maybe not, but you'll do it yourself."

Then he told me about the delicate clutch that lies hidden between the conscious and unconscious minds. He showed me how to release this clutch and relieve my pain. I did as he told me, shot my arm over my head, and my shoulder into place.

As I walked out of that house I was filled with grateful wonder for the power that had been revealed to me. I marvelled as I watched Smith the carpenter take himself off, without pay, to his work in the country. There was a snappy stride to his short legs, an independent rhythm to his stocky body, and a graceful swing to his saws and jack-planes. And I thought of another Carpenter who had lived on the shores of Galilee. Maybe, if the truth were known, their methods would not be found so far removed.

I had occasion a few years later to test the carpenter's formula again. This time my life was at stake. I was caught in a blizzard in the Nevada mountains. I had been stripping a ledge and hadn't noticed the temperature drop, so absorbed in my work was I, nor the black clouds coming up, before the icy gale struck me, almost keeling me over. Snow was flying as fine and as hard as sand. I looked around, nearly blinded by the whirl, wondering how I should get to my camp, which was less than a mile away. Should I dare venture down the mountain? The hole I was digging offered a little shelter, although it was scarcely four feet deep. "I can't stay here," I thought, "I'll freeze before morning." Then the fear of death seized me. "I must get to the camp," I heard myself say. I started down on my hands and knees, but had not gone more than fifty yards when I felt myself in a sea of floating snow, without sense of direction. Panic-stricken, I struggled back to the hole I had just left. My pick and shovel were already buried, and I had to gopher to find them. The cold was becoming so intense that my hands had little feeling in them as I set about to dig a narrow hole in the wall of the one already dug. I worked desperately, for night was setting in and the snow continued to come down like bounding waves. The crash of falling trees sent tremors along the hillside. At last I had the hole dug far enough in the wall. I would be protected from the snow, yet I had little hope of being alive in the morning. I crawled into the cramped hole, shivering in every particle of me and my teeth chattering beyond control. I whittled at the handle of the pick, hoping to kindle a tiny fire with the shavings, but my sulphur matches were too wet to light. Then in utter despair I crumbled up like a land urchin and awaited the end. A feeling of numbness came over me; my eyes grew drowsy. I shook myself, knowing quite well what this drowsiness meant. The coyotes would be feasting on me by to-morrow night. Then, like a flash, the stocky form of Smith the carpenter seemed to loom up before me. Would that clutch that he had told me about—that delicate hair-trigger thing that lay between the two minds—would that work here? Somehow, I don't know why, I felt a glow come over me. It was like the warmth from an unobserved electric heater. I cannot say that I was comfortable, yet I was no longer acutely conscious of cold. Nor was sleep trying to best me. And the strangest part of that experience was that the night seemed to pass away quickly. When daylight came the sky was clear, the air crisp and invigorating. I rolled myself out on to the snow and started down the mountain-side. Without searching for my camp I kept on down to the valley below, and kept on going—nor did I ever go back to that mountain again.

I will relate one other experience with the carpenter's clutch. I was placer mining at that time on the Picaune River in northern California. My nearest neighbour was about eighteen miles away. Seldom did I ever see a human being, but there were bears, and coyotes, and rattlesnakes in plenty.

I had been working over a month, ground sluicing for a little gold. One afternoon I stripped a piece of the serpentine bed-rock. In the crevice lay the heavy gold, and I had my tools ready to gouge it out. I shut the water off at the bulkhead and eagerly ran back to my work. So keen was I to hoke the gold out of the seams that I had no regard for time. I worked like a beaver until night set in. Then I thought I'd get to my camp, a short distance away. So I gathered up my gold, elated indeed, for I had about nine hundred dollars worth in the poke. My camp consisted of a small tent; outside was an open fire and a Dutch cook oven. I threw the poke into the tent and reached for the

THE CARPENTER'S CLUTCH

axe to cut some kindling wood. The night was dark; I was excited after my haul, and I let the axe slip. It slashed my wrist—a deep gash. When I got the candle lit, I saw that I had opened an artery. With every beat of my heart the blood spouted up like a geyser. My heart pulsed in rapid panicky strokes as I realized my situation. To reach a doctor I would have to cross two mountains: one was three thousand feet above me, and beyond that was China Mountain, nine thousand feet high. The doctor was at the town of Weed, sixty miles away. I was bleeding to death, and something had to be done quickly, so I cut a rope off one of the tent-poles and marled this around my arm above the wound. I thought I had made a sailor job of it, but the blood kept coming. Then I wrapped yard after yard of a stripped sheet around the wrist. Still I could not stop the flow of blood. By this time I was near the point of nervous exhaustion, and my heart kept pounding. Was I going to slip my moorings there on the Picaune River? At the rate that life was ebbing I knew it would not take long to run out. Then I became conscious of a severe pain in my arm. It was swelling, as the tent-rope cut into the flesh. If only I could get hold of the severed artery and tie it. I unwound the sheet and dug my fingers into the wound. What a red mess I was when at last I gave up trying to catch hold of the artery! Overcome then by a feeling of nausea, I threw myself on my willow bunk. There I struggled to face death, unreconciled to my fate. In the deep silence of the mountains, my thoughts turned hither and thither, seeking some outlet. Then again there flashed upon me the message of Smith the carpenter. Could I reach the clutch between the two minds before it was too late? I knew there lay a source of power within me, but here was I at the utmost extremity, different from any I had ever known before—I was bleeding to death.

I surrendered my will to the unconscious self. At once I felt myself grow calm; fear left me. My heart began to beat slowly and steadily, and I noticed that the flow of blood grew less. I raised myself out of the bunk, feeling quite strong. Placing my arm in a sling, I started up the mountain in the dark of that June night. Cautiously I crept through the greasewood, listening as I went for the warning of the rattlesnake. When I reached the top of the mountain I could see a camp fire six or seven miles away. My strength still held out and I made for it. I found there two forest rangers. When they had heard my tale they offered me a horse, and I rode on to the doctor's, arriving there at nine o'clock the next morning. The doctor laughed incredulously when I told him I had severed an artery.

"You couldn't have travelled sixty miles," he said, "with an open artery."

"Cut off the bandages," I urged, "and see for yourself."

He was dumbfounded when he saw the wound. It was not even congealed, but looked fresh and

THE CARPENTER'S CLUTCH

angry. He reached in with his forceps, caught the ends of the artery and tied them up. After sewing seven stitches in my wrist he turned me loose. In three days those stitches were taken out and I went back to my gold and my camp on the Picaune.

There may be minds that will scoff at the childish simplicity of my belief. Yet I must have reverence for that which brings me cheer in darkest hours. My prayer, or wish, or formula, is simple enough. It works well for me. I commit the ills of the flesh—and the spirit also—to the unconscious mind, and through this channel get in touch with some great source that I know nothing about. I wouldn't moralize on the subject, and I'm not a religious man. I merely speak for myself of life as I know it—thirty-five years of ups and downs.

CHAPTER NINETEEN

EASY PICKINGS

I HAVE wandered far from the tale of those days immediately after I had left the San Francisco bay schooner, a victim of malarial fever. One afternoon as I was wandering along the water-front looking at the ships of many nations and wondering if a sea voyage would help me, a round and red-faced man of about forty, wearing a straw hat and a tweed suit, walked up to me and asked me for a light for his cigar. Then he began to talk to me, and seemed kind and sympathetic. Little did I know that I was talking to one of the worst crooks in San Francisco.

He became communicative as we stood there, and told me that his poor wife was sick, up in Vancouver; he turned from me as he spoke with his handkerchief to his eyes.

"If I can only get to her before she dies," he said. "Every minute is precious, and I am a stranger here."

"I am a stranger too," I said, "but I ought to be able to find a ship for you." I felt very sorry for this tender-hearted man whose wife was dying, hundreds of miles away. My own troubles sank into nothingness compared to his.

EASY PICKINGS

He was grateful, and assured me that money was nothing to him. He even pulled out a roll of bills and asked me to help myself. Of course I refused, for it was a pleasure to help him. It never occurred to me that the bills might be "phoney."

At the Pacific Mail dock I learned that a steamer was leaving the following day for Victoria, B.C., on which he would be able to get passage. He said that he would go back later for his ticket, and urging me to at least let him treat me to a glass of beer, skilfully guided me into a saloon of his choice.

"Now," said he on the way, "you must let me help you to some money. I doubt if you have much."

"Oh, yes, I have a little," I said bashfully.

Quick as a flash he asked me how much I had, and I, taken unawares, answered like a fool and told him that I had two hundred and forty dollars. His eyes sparkled and his stride lengthened. We entered the saloon.

The bar-room was small. Its only occupant was the bar-tender, who was long and lanky, with a face that might have been chiselled out of marble, so pale and inscrutable it was. He was an opium fiend, I discovered later, well known, and sometimes protected by the police.

"What will you have?" he asked as my seeming friend and I approached the bar.

"I'll take steam beer," said I.

"Ditto for me," said the crook as he flung a gold eagle on the bar.

The beer being served, the bar-tender excused himself, to go and get change, he said. I offered to pay, but he said that he needed the change, anyway. I didn't know that this was all part of the play: that the stage was set and that now another character was about to make his appearance for my sole benefit.

As we drank our beer a door opened from a back room into the bar, letting in an elderly man whose hair and beard were greying. He wore a long linen overall and a slouch hat.

"Have a drink with us, old fellow," said my friend.

"No, sir," answered the old man with a strong Western twang. "I buy my own drinks, and pay for 'em."

"Oh, very well, if that's the way you feel about it. I'll just shake the dice with you and see who pays for the three of us."

Enter Mr. Hophead, bar-tender.

"Give us the dice," challenged the old man. "How will we shake?"

"Tops and bottoms, three dice."

"Never heard of such a thing," whined the old Westerner, "but I'll try anything once, to be sociable. Now, how does that game of yourn go?"

I was bristling with interest. This was something I had not run across before, and the three crooks knew that I was about ready to nibble at the bait. I might have been saved if that was all I did, but

EASY PICKINGS

instead I insisted on swallowing hook, line, and pole.

"The game is simple," said my genial friend whose wife was dying in Vancouver. "Take those three dice, put them in the box, rattle and roll. Guess the numbers on top and bottom, add them up, and the one who guesses closest is the one who drinks free beer."

"Gosh a'mighty! I'll take a whack at you, anyway," and the old man unbuttoned the long overall. I stood by, feeling sorry for myself that I wasn't asked to join in this wonderful game of dice.

The old fellow rattled the bones.

"Before you throw them on the bar," said my companion, with a winsome smile, "we must both make a guess."

"All right, I'll guess twenty-seven, and, damn my old skin, I'll bet you ten dollars and beer!"

"You're certainly on," chimed the other, digging into his pocket for money. "My guess will be twenty-one."

The money was up, the game was on. The bartender and I looked on as the dice rolled.

"Count the numbers!" shouted old Linen Duster excitedly, "and Gol darn you count them right!"

My companion won. Tossing the ten dollars to me, he said:

"Here, take the old hayseed's money. I have more than I need."

"No, no," I said, "I wasn't in on your game. The money is yours." I tossed it back again.

Had I been a little more intelligent I would have noticed that the bar-tender sighed and the old man retreated through the door by which he had entered, in a sort of routine way. This fact passed me by at the moment, but the memory of it has often recurred.

The trap was now ready to spring, and I was to be my own hangman. We hang ourselves many times in life with the hemp rope of our greed.

My friend turned to me and eagerly whispered: "You see how the game works, don't you?" He picked up the three dice in his fingers. "No matter which way you count them top and bottom, there's always twenty-one; seven on each dice."

Surely I was green and dense.

"I can't understand it yet," said I, getting terribly excited. I was afraid that old Linen Duster might come back and spoil my chance of ever knowing. Then he explained as if he were talking to a child, that if there was a six on top, one was always on the bottom; if four, then three on the bottom—always seven, top and bottom.

The old man walked into the bar again, holding a fat-looking purse in his hand. "The loss of that money don't hurt me so very much, stranger," he said, striding over to the bar. He opened the purse. It was full of what appeared to be twenty-dollar gold pieces. It wasn't gold at all, I learned afterwards, but souvenirs of the mid-winter fair in San Francisco.

"I'll shake with anyone here for three hundred

EASY PICKINGS

dollars, but don't think that if I lose it will break me."

My companion nudged me. "Here's your chance," he whispered. "Go after him. Put up your two hundred and forty and I'll lend you sixty more. It's easy money."

There was no chance to lose that I could see. I put up my money, all I had in the world, and sixty more.

"Now, you shake the dice," said my opponent. "You certainly look honest to me. Rattle them, roll them, throw them on the bar."

"I'm a-guessing twenty," he continued.

"I guess twenty-one," I cried, and wouldn't have given one dollar for all his three hundred, so sure was I of winning. Well, I rattled and rolled the bones, feeling sorry for the old man all the time. Then I counted them. I counted them again. The numbers top and bottom amounted to only twenty!

I was aware of the bar-tender smiling cynically to himself in the mirror, smiling at the sucker, who like the dreamer pervades society from the highest to the lowest strata. I was aware that the old man had quietly pocketed my earnings, leaving me only a few coppers to my name. I saw the other crook deliberately slide out of a side door. I felt myself to be alone, with possibility for vengeance gone from me. Still I stood in the bare and silent room, staring, staring at the dice on the mahogany bar, realizing at last the trick of substitution that had taken from me all I had.

The psychology of being a good loser is the feeling that the hurts of to-day may be the cause of winning to-morrow's fight. I went out of that saloon as if I were bent on urgent business, and I was. By now it was plain enough to me that my time would be lost in seeking redress. The matter of the moment was food, shelter, and occupation. I had no time to think of malaria and the chills that would get me soon. The past was obscured by the dawn of the morrow.

CHAPTER TWENTY

STEAMER LIGHTS

THE cream-coloured November sun had only a little way to go before night would come sweeping in its wake. I walked along the water-front and watched the ships swinging limply in the undertow. That same evening I found a ship, the barque *Ferris S. Thompson*, bound for Seattle for coal, and returning again to San Francisco.

This good luck was due to a sailor whom I had befriended when I was master of the bay schooner. I had been unloading coal one afternoon in San Francisco. He had come on board and asked me if I could give him some work to do.

"I'm sorry," said I, "I can't give you work."

He turned away without another word and walked ashore. I stopped shovelling coal and looked after him. Then I thought that it hadn't been so long ago since I was adrift, too—with no money, no friends, no work, and the cruel feeling that nobody cared. I knew that I had gold in my pocket, and I wondered how long I should have it. Then I called after him:

"Hey, there! Come on back here! I want to see you!"

He turned and came.

"You're broke," said I.

"Yes, and hungry into the bargain."

"Here's ten dollars for you."

He thanked me and walked away, and I went on shovelling coal.

That had been five months before, and this evening, from where he stood on the forecastle head of the barque, he recognized me on the wharf. He was the second mate and the barque needed one man. I got the job. Well repaid I was for the small service I had rendered him. One is usually well repaid for a kind deed.

Years later, at a time when I had plenty of money, I was walking one afternoon in Stanley Park, Vancouver. I noticed a young man sitting on a bench looking pale and hungry and sad.

"What's your trouble?" I asked. "Tell me. I've noticed you sitting here for the past two hours. Maybe I can help."

He cleared his throat and a wistful smile shadowed his lips.

"I'm broke," he said, "and hungry. I've been sleeping in the park for the last three nights and I'm just about sick."

"How did you get in for this?"

"I put what money I had into a mine up in the country," waving his hand towards the north. "I thought there was more to it than there was. There was nothing."

STEAMER LIGHTS

I paid his room and board for a week and gave him twenty dollars.

Years later I met him again. This time it was I who was down and out, sick with rheumatism left to me when the Goldfield smash had stripped me of a fortune.

I had been riding on a lumber wagon all one day trying to get to the little town of Manhattan, Nevada. Five miles out of town the wagon broke down, and crippled as I was, I had to walk that distance. Not a soul did I know there. Imagine my surprise when I arrived in town—sick, broke, and hungry—to find the man I had helped in Stanley Park. He recognized me at once, and my condition also.

"Now," he said kindly, taking me by the arm, "it's my turn to help you." He led me to his tent, sent for a doctor, and kept me with him until I was well again.

Then there was the Chinaman on the Fraser River who ran the fan-tan house at Stevestown. One night as I passed his door I rescued him from three fishermen who were beating him up. Later I met him in Vancouver as I stood at a street corner wondering what to do next, after a turn of ill luck. I spotted him walking along on the other side of the street, but he did not seem to see me. He walked by, crossed the street, and approached me slowly. Then with outstretched hand, "How do you do?" he said rather indifferently. After the usual limp Oriental handshake he passed on as if he had never seen me, without waiting for a word. But he left in my hand three twenty-dollar gold pieces.

As to the barque *Ferris S. Thompson*, from which I have strayed so far: the voyage was a very long one for so short a distance. The captain was a State of Maine man, and old at that. His only worry at sea was an inborn fear of steamships. He thought that he was in constant danger of being run down by one of them.

He held high regard for sailing-ship masters, but none for the captains of steamers. Even in daylight if he saw a steamer he would alter his course and steer away from the distant smoke. When nights set in everyone on board was made miserable. If he saw a masthead light, regardless of his position, he would roar:

"Tack ship, stand by the headsails, weather fore and main braces. Har-r-r-d-a-le-e-eee!"

Around we'd go on another tack. He'd stand trembling on the poop until the steamer's light faded into the distance. Three months vanished on that voyage, although the distance round trip was but two thousand miles.

Finally, after dodging, so it seemed, every steamer that plied the coast-line of the North Pacific, we reached San Francisco. What a welcome we were given! On the wharf, as the tug-boat breasted the barque alongside, stood the managing owner. No sooner were we within hailing distance than his voice reached out to us, and it had the same effect

STEAMER LIGHTS

on every man—it was as though we were caught aback in a squall.

"Get off that ship, every one of you! I don't want you even to make her fast to the wharf!" Then aft to the old captain: "Where have you been—to China? Gone three months instead of six weeks!" The language that followed was of that rare order known only to masters, mates, and owners.

He paid us all off then and there, with no good wishes for our future, for to him each and all of us were equally guilty. The old captain took his medicine like the rest of us. What did he care for the abuse of an owner, compared to the sharp stem of a steamer?

But just by changing ships he was not able to get away from steamers. Five years later I was mate on a ship bound north for Seattle and we passed the barque *Oakland*. This same old captain had commanded her—but not that day. He, with the crew, had taken to the boats twenty-four hours before. The manless barque was left to the mercy of wind and wave.

I pleaded with my captain to let me take her and sail her into Puget Sound, for she was loaded with lumber, and I felt sure that I could salvage her, although she was waterlogged. The captain would not hear of it, and the salvage fell to an ocean-going tug which chanced upon her, towed her into port and received one hundred and twenty thousand dollars salvage. I have often regretted that I didn't defy the captain and sail her to port or die in the attempt.

The captain and crew were picked up off Cape Disappointment, the story being that the barque *Oakland* had been abandoned because she was so leaky. But I knew, and the captain knew, that other reason—STEAMERS!

CHAPTER TWENTY-ONE

SAILS AND SAILORS

From now on I will summon the memories of my voyages, letting them wash ashore on a ground swell from the deep. In the nooky inlet where the driftwood lies, I shall gather together the pieces that are worth salvaging from out of the kelp, and carry them to the high-water mark, dropping them there.

Seven years of sailing had crowded out the self-conscious thoughts of youth and developed in me the riper side of the man. I could appraise life now, refusing to be beaten by its vagaries. If I happened to be without a ship or without money in my pocket, I knew it was all in the day's work. The smiling seas were mine to-day—lee shores belonged to yesterday.

I had a great ambition to become a master of ships as well as a master of men; but I had to wait, first to become a citizen of the United States, and then to get the necessary sea experience to qualify. Nautical astronomy and the rules of sailing I was thoroughly familiar with. However, I still had much to learn about the ways of human nature.

I was in a Puget Sound port and my money was getting low, when I met the hare-lipped captain.

He was loading lumber for San Francisco. He held a half-interest in a three-topmast schooner, the other half being held by a Dutchman in San Francisco who ran a coffee-royal house for the benefit of sailors who mixed their brandy with the Dutchman's black coffee.

When I met the captain he was coming out of a saloon on his way to the schooner. He was short-tacking along the sidewalk and had great difficulty in heading towards the wharf.

"Do you need any sailors?" I asked him.

"I do," he hiccoughed, "but if I stop now to tell you what I want I'll fall down. Come on, take me by the arm, and steer me to the schooner."

This was not easy; he was too heavy to keep an even keel. But I put him on board and in his cabin, and he invited me to remain for supper. It was unusual for a sailor to eat with the master of a ship, but I allowed for his condition, for when a man is drunk he wants company to listen to his boasting.

The ship's cook, who had one eye and a drooping moustache, brought in the supper. He spread it noisily, and with one nervous glance at me, bounded forward to the galley. I learned afterwards that even the mates were afraid to face the captain that night.

As I sat opposite him I thought that he might be a hard man to handle if things went wrong. But he treated me very well and told me to come down in the morning; he would ship me as a sailor.

Now it seemed to me, who had so often been a

SAILS AND SAILORS

victim of leaky ships, that I might ask a justifiable question. I asked:

"How is this ship for leaking, captain?"

That question proved to be my undoing.

"What did you say?" he inquired fiercely. "Just say that again! Just say that again, if you dare! My ship leaky!" Then without hesitation, with a single movement of his arm, he picked up a large platter of fried steak and flung it at me, just missing my face. His language was startling even to me, and before I could move he was up and peeling off his coat.

Discretion seemed preferable to a show-down just then, and I made a leap for the deck, where the two mates stood grinning as I shot by them to the wharf. I did manage to call to the mate, "I'll be with you in the morning, sir," before I ducked behind a lumber pile. None too soon, for the captain's head showed above the companion-way. Then he treated the helpless mates to the language intended for me.

Bright and early the next morning I was aboard the hare-lipped captain's ship. He had no recollection of having hired me, but hired me over again, and I helped load ship for the four days we were in port. The captain was drunk all the time and very disagreeable, especially to the mate. The result was that the mate left, and we sailed without any first officer.

There were six men in the forecastle: big, raw-boned Scandinavian sailors, and the second mate was apparently a good sailor, but not a navigator.

Plying in coastwise trade he did not require a second mate's licence. Two days out at sea, the captain, who did all his drinking ashore and carried no rum with him, became delirious for the want of it. The sailors were uneasy and scented disaster. When the topsails blew away they held a consultation and decided that the captain must be locked up if we were ever to reach port. But the question was, who of us had the nerve to seize him and tie him up.

The cook was called into conference. The crew thought that he, being in close touch with the raving captain, could coax him into his cabin and quickly lock the door. I'll never forget the expression on the cook's face when this proposition was made to him.

As I said before, he had one eye. The loss of the other had the tendency to protrude the good one, which seemed to bulge out on his cheek. He had a three-day growth of sandy beard. The drooping moustache, which was about three shades darker, covered his mouth, and when he spoke it was self-consciously, with one dough-spattered finger to his mouth. But there was no hesitation about his words: he could not and would not lock up the captain.

It was six o'clock in the afternoon of the third day at sea. The wind was coming stronger, and the spanker should have been reefed. The topsails, what was left of them, were flying in long strips at the masthead. The captain was sitting on a mooring-bitt alongside the man at the wheel, counting and counting on his fingers. Often he would spring to his feet, clawing at some imaginary bug crawling on his coat collar. No one dared speak to him, least of all the second mate. He was doubly scared—of the captain, and of what might happen to the ship, for he knew enough to dread many things and not enough to save the ship from one of them.

Suddenly and quietly the captain sprang for the helmsman and started to beat him. The sailor was a heavy man, but the attack was too sudden, and he had no chance to come back. He began to cry " Murder."

Two Swedish sailors and I ran for the poop deck, and got there not a moment too soon. We pulled the captain away from the helmsman just in time to prevent him from throwing the man overboard. The captain turned on me with unleashed fury, but the three of us soon mastered him and buckled him down the companion-way and into his room. There we locked him in, after first removing anything that he might injure himself with. By this time he was raving like a wild animal.

On deck I asked the mate if he knew his position of ship or where he was on the ocean. He knew no more about it than did the sailors in the forecastle.

We called a council again, and I told the crew that while I held no licence I felt sure I could make San Francisco, since I could navigate a ship. They agreed that I should command her, and I took the captain's sextant. The following day I found our bearings and headed for the Golden Gate.

For two days the captain howled and raged. He was so vicious that no one dared go into his room, but fortunately he did not try to escape. The cook fed him through the porthole with a long-handled dipper full of gruel, strongly flavoured with Lea and Perrins' sauce. When I asked him why he did this he laughed at my ignorance of the sobering-up properties of this sauce. I learned later that long-shoremen and mule-skinners have also discovered this valuable secret.

After the second day the captain's condition improved and he slept more. On the sixth day we sailed into San Francisco Bay, and I was just about to come to anchor when he demanded to be released and allowed on the deck of his own schooner. I refused his demand, thinking that he was weak and should have a doctor. Without more argument he withdrew his head from the porthole, threw his strength against the door, smashed it to splinters, and came up on deck as if nothing had happened.

He surveyed the harbour with a sweep of his eye, and inquired with a flame of oaths what I was doing with his ship.

"I'm going to anchor her," I said, trying to put on a brave front.

"Never mind the anchor. I'm going to take her alongside the wharf. Lower the jibs down and drop the spanker."

I was about to protest, thinking that if he were to

sail her alongside the wharf he would tear the sides out of her, but discipline held me in its iron grip. I wondered if he could possibly do it. He did. He sailed up to Mission Flats and abreast the Fourth Street bridge. He pointed the schooner in towards the wharf as if she were alone on the water.

There were tug-boats, ferry-boats, bay scows, and sailing craft of all kinds and descriptions tooting and shouting and screaming for the right of way. Our captain, if he saw them, paid no attention, but took his wheel, and with his eye on the wharf, sailed in. It so happened that there was a vacant berth at the end of the pier, ahead of which lay a number of Greek fishing boats. They saw us coming and scurried out of the way like a flock of sheep, for it looked as if there would be a nasty crash.

"Drop the peak of the fore and mainsail and let the jib go by the run!" shouted the captain. When this was done the wind fluttered out of our sails, and the schooner crept lazily in, gliding alongside, harmlessly squashing the barnacles on the piles, to the amazement of the crew and the crowd gathered on the dock.

"Make her fast, and lower the fore and mainsail! Then get ashore and get your money!" ordered the captain. That was his acknowledgment to us for our help and our silence.

In the Dutchman's coffee-house where we were paid off we were all friends again, and there the captain was able to get drunk once more: as drunk as possible. When I left them the captain was surrounded by his loving crew, who chanted his praise in cognac whispers, while the cook reclined against the hare-lipped chief with an arm around his neck.

CHAPTER TWENTY-TWO

AND CAPTAINS

At the age of twenty-three I became a citizen of the United States, took my examination, and passed for mate. My first ship as an officer was bound for Australia. I knew now the tricks of sailors: their hatreds, their sympathies, their childish joys and youthful egotisms.

It is a common saying at sea, especially among the officers and masters who graduate from apprentice seamanship to their commands, that few men who start in the forecastle ever reach the bridge. Yet I am convinced that the men who work their way up know how to handle men the better for having been one of them. The commander must know and understand the nature of his men: show them consideration by listening to their petty grievances, and show appreciation even though they make mistakes.

I have found that this rule works on land as well as on the sea. The man who is not in close touch with his employees, preferring to remain aloof and issuing his orders through some prejudiced foreman, is usually in trouble with his men.

During the World War I worked in the Submarine

Boat Corporation's yard—the second largest shipyard in the United States. As many as twenty-five thousand men were employed there. The number of men discharged every day was astounding: it seemed to me that the reason lay with their foreman, who did not understand or want to know them. I was Superintendent of Ship Rigging and Outfitting, and I was proud of the fact that for more than a year I had no occasion to fire a man, and all that time my department was above standard in efficiency. To choose a man you must be able to size him up. Then having chosen him you must treat him with the consideration due him.

The voyage to Australia was a pleasant one, although it seemed disappointing to the captain. He shipped me as mate more on my physical appearance than for any other reason, for he wanted a man who could fight. I understood from the ship's carpenter, who had sailed many voyages with him, that there was usually trouble aboard his ship. That voyage there was no fighting and very little growling, and yet the men were the average types that are picked up in any seaport.

"Don't get too friendly with them," the captain warned me. "I know them. One of these days they will be kicking you into the lee scuppers. That's the way they repay kindness."

"We'll see," said I optimistically.

I was young, but I knew the sailor's temperament. When I spoke to them it was to call them by their names, and not by some hit-or-miss name with an oath.

The crew was musical. There were a baritone, a trombonist, and a cornet player in the forecastle. One of them made a triangle out of a chain hook, and the orchestra was complete. During the dog watches in the tropics, and on Sundays, we played our best. At times I would spell the cornet player off and play with them.

It was all a bit hard on the captain, who had no ear for music, and so made no allowance for varied harmonies. When the sounds reached him on the poop deck, he'd pull at his pipe and finger his beard, pacing the deck on the double quick. One evening, while we were sailing south of the Samoas, we ran into a head-wind. It was rather unusual, for the south-east trades should have held out for another five degrees south.

We were playing that evening when the wind hauled ahead and pushed the ship off her course. The captain came running from the poop forward. "Now, see what you've done!" he roared. "Cut that music out and cut it out for good! I knew something would happen with that clabbering going on."

This was only the opening shot. We were treated to even more abusive accusations. The forecastle orchestra was blamed for the head-wind, and the instruments had to be put away. The sailor who beat time on the chain-hook triangle hung it up over his bunk for drying his socks. That settled music for that voyage. The men wouldn't even sing a capstan chantey when they were heaving up the anchor. It took nine months to make the voyage, and at the end I left the ship, and so did the crew.

On another voyage I had quite a contrary experience. I was still in the forecastle. The mate wanted music in the air. If you lifted a rope yarn from the deck you were to put a chantey to it. The mate was big and tough and a terrible fighter, and enforced his musical inclinations on a shrinking crew. They were afraid of him, and sang for all they were worth at his bidding, regardless of mood or weather, and weather means mood to a sailor. Once it was cold and blowing and the heart of the forecastle was lower than the barometer. But the mate wanted a song.

"Take a pull at the lee fore braces!" he shouted, and the shivering crew caught hold. But the song was not there.

The mate walked up to the first man, who happened to be a Russian Finn. "Sing, damn you!" he ordered, with a wallop over the Finn's head. The sailor, miserably defending himself from the blow, clapped his hands to his head, squirming. Then he burst forth into the melody of Ranzo, but the words that came were hardly in keeping with the tune:

"Oh, Jesus-Christ-Al-mi-i-ghty," moaned the Finn, in harmonious rhythm, while "Ranzo boys, Ranzo," chorused the crew.

There was another captain I sailed with as mate. He was an old man past sixty, but supple and a wonderful ratter. It was seldom, if ever, that a rat got away from him. He detested them so that as a result there was unusual cordiality between him and his crew, oiling the wheels of discipline.

The captain wore false teeth, and whenever he lay down for a nap he would take them out and put them on a stool beside the bed. One night as we were on our way to the South Seas, a bold rat stole the lower set. Everyone aboard ship was accused impartially of having stolen them, and every man was searched. But the teeth could not be found. I being among the accused, and anxious to clear myself, suggested that it might have been a rat. The captain was hard put to answer without the teeth and he lisped badly.

"What in hell would a rat want with them?" he snapped. "It ain't any rat." Once started he went on swearing with unforgettable variety, while we continued to turn the cabin inside out in our search for the teeth. Suddenly a rat ran out from the storeroom.

"Look!" I shouted, "there he goes!"

The Old Man's eyes blazed red and he munched his gums together.

"Shut the companion door," he roared, and I slammed it to with a bang.

Then commenced the most vicious attack on a rat that I have ever seen. The captain peeled off his clothes as a precaution against the rat running up his trouser leg, and armed with belaying pins we chased the rat around the cabin, knocking dents in the teakwood as we missed him. That was nothing to the old captain. Naked and sweating, he cursed the rat as he ran around after him. For about an hour we kept up the running fight. News had spread through the ship and stealthy footsteps on deck heralded the bearded faces that looked solemnly through the skylight at us, shoving each other aside from time to time in perfect silence. The rat managed to disappear.

"Go on deck," ordered the captain, "and look after the ship. That damned rat has got my teeth for good. I'm going to have a sleep."

He lay down exhausted, not even turning down the cabin light. I knew he felt terribly about his teeth. The port in the Fijis to which we were bound was small, and held out no hope there for new teeth. About the only pleasure the old fellow had was sprucing up to go ashore with the dignity suitable to the master of a full-rigged ship, and one of his most absorbing toilet preparations had been the pumice-stoning of those teeth, comparable to the manner in which he had his decks squeegeed and holy-stoned. I knew how much he must be suffering down there in his bunk, and I too cursed the ship's rats.

Half an hour must have passed. Then there was a terrible rumpus in the cabin: swift shadows pelted across the skylight, and I could hear a seaman's profanity coming through the bulkhead.

AND CAPTAINS

Then followed absolute quiet. I tiptoed down, and there stood the Old Man naked as the day he was born, holding a wriggling rat up by the tail.

"You infernal sneak you, what did you do with my teeth?" he was asking the rat. Receiving no answer, he swung the rat's head against the stairway and flung him out and overboard.

I asked him if it was the same rat we had both been after. He said it was, and then he told me how the rat, sensing danger when we were chasing him, crawled up under the stool at the head of the bed where the captain's false teeth had been kept. There he stayed until everything seemed quiet, then took a peep out from under the seat of the stool and—stared right into the eye of the captain! How long they glared at each other, or how they measured one another, I do not know, but when the fight began it was no easy one, to judge from the looks of the Old Man, whose scratches it took several inches of plaster to calk.

Two days later the cook found the captain's teeth in a rat's nest near a sack of potatoes, and after that there was no cat or terrier that could equal him in his sniffing and scratching. He never left his teeth on the stool again, but slept with them under his pillow.

CHAPTER TWENTY-THREE

SUPERSTITIONS

Captains of sailing ships used to have time to sit around and watch for omens of Fate. Sometimes they were even more superstitious than sailors before the mast. Although they were supposed to have a higher degree of intelligence, they came in contact with more traditions of the sea and were very susceptible to them.

Once I was mate with a Swedish captain who believed that to see whales was a bad omen; he claimed that gales of wind would follow, and I have to admit that while I was with him this was more or less true.

Another, a Dane, believed that when he dreamed of white horses we were sure to have a blow, and as he seemed to be always dreaming of them, and predicting disaster in the mildest of weather, I did not stay long with him. There was no barometer on board, nor would he allow any, for some reason known best to himself.

I made two voyages with another twisted old warp of a man, before we finally lost the ship. He was afraid of his shadow. He would never allow another shadow to cross it. This required considerable side-

SUPERSTITIONS

stepping, especially around noon when we would be taking the sun together. I, out of devilry, would throw my shadow across his.

"See what you're doing now," he would roar. "What can you expect with this kind of work going on?"

I'd excuse myself and separate the shadows, but he would be deeply depressed for a long time.

He had queer ideas about booms and ladders, being afraid to pass under them, and so kept continually dodging. When the sea was afire with phosphorescent glow, and the spray would lift up tiny diamond blue bulbs to the deck, he would murmur: "Yes, by heavens, there's something back of this!"

The ship he commanded was old, and because of its lack of buoyancy only fit to carry lumber, which can stand more water than any other cargo. We were loading at Garden City, Oregon, and had just shipped a new crew, when the men discovered they were aboard a leaky ship.

They turned out and left; the next crew also; and before we had the ship loaded we had recruited six crews. The last, you might say, was shanghaied. These men came from Portland, Oregon, and were lime-juice sailors. The moment they put their bags on board the tug pulled us out to anchor. There we could hold them until we were ready for sea.

When the anchor was down I called on them to pump her out, saying to encourage them: "She hasn't been pumped out for several days, and you may find a little water in her."

This wasn't true, for while we were at the wharf I had kept two longshoremen busy pumping her most of the time, and it had been difficult to get even them to do it, so bad was her reputation.

There was a tall, slim Irishman in the crew, who became at once the spokesman for the others.

"Ah," said he with a smile, "and shure it won't take *us* no time at all, at all, to pump her out for ye."

I smiled too, a different smile, and looked out at the bar we were soon to cross on our way to the open sea. The lime-juice crew pumped for an hour with never a suck from the pump. I could hear them growling and swearing. Presently the Irishman stuck his head above the deck load and shouted to me:

"Bejasus, and has the bottom dropped out of her? Is it a ship we're on at all, at all, or is it just a raft of lumber? The divil himself wouldn't go to sea on her!"

It wasn't so much what the Irishman said that made me roar with laughter, it was his expression —that of an abandoned castaway. I nearly lost all my new-made dignity of coastwise mate then and there.

I told him that I thought the little water that washed in the bilges was a small matter, and that a few strokes more of the pump would settle it. He crawled down to the pump again, but not before he had said a few words:

SUPERSTITIONS

" It's perpetual motion ye'd ought to have on the pumps. As God is me judge, I belave ye could see the fish in the ocean through the bottom of her!"

They were still pumping when the superstitious captain came on board. His expression was a good deal like the Irishman's—clabby and dearing

" Did you hear the news before you left the wharf?" he muttered nervously.

" Hear what?" I asked.

He put his hand to his mouth. " Sh—listen! The rats left the ship this morning between four and five o'clock!"

" Did you see them leave?" I asked, suppressing a grin.

" I didn't. But there were others that saw them. Swarming off in droves, they were . . ."

" I'll tell yez," came a furious voice, as the Irishman's head appeared again, " I'll tell yez once and for all, there isn't any bottom in the bloody auld hooker! It's murder ye'd be doing to have dacinct men sign articles on a rotten auld hulk without ribs or anything to hold her together!"

The captain wet his lips with his long red tongue. He looked at me uncertainly, then his eyes shifted to the Irishman, and he sighed heavily. For a moment there was a lull—even the pumps stopped. The breakers that scattered on the sprits of the bar had an ominous gnawing sound, in that moment of intense rat superstition. Then the Irishman spoke again, deliberately, finally:

" There isn't wan of us will sail wid yez. We're

sailors, every wan of us, but we're not web-footed. Did yez hear that now? And the divil a foot will we put on yere ship!"

The ultimatum seemed to strike as much consternation in the heart of the captain as if the crew could do otherwise than sail, seeing they were already on the ship.

"Is she leaking any worse?" he asked.

"I think she is," I answered, at the same time turning my back on the Irishman, for it would never do to let him hear about the rats.

"I know where it is," and the captain looked wildly about him. "It's that damned stern post again. I've been calking it off and on for the last ten years."

He took off his hat and rubbed his bald head, apparently thinking deeply. Undoubtedly the rats knew about that old leak in the sternpost. Why then should they desert their old nests after all these years? It was an old leak with a new aspect.

The lime-juice crew had stopped working and stood around the mainmast talking, their voices rasping and twanging.

Toot! toot! toot! came the tug-boat, none too soon.

At once the captain applied ship's dignity to a bad situation.

"I'll put her on the dry dock next trip," he promised, " but we'll have to get to sea with her now. I'll talk to the crew."

He walked forward with a brave front, for he

didn't want to go to sea with her any more than the crew did, but for him it was a choice between the risk and giving up his command, not to mention the jibes of other captains, his drinking mates ashore. With the crew it was simply risk, and it is always wrong to take discontented men to sea.

He talked to them kindly, singing the praises of his ship, and their argument was fortunately cut short by the tug-boat captain, who unfeelingly demanded why he should be forced to wait all day on a bunch of good-for-nothing loafers.

So we heaved up the anchor, taking the tow-line aboard, and soon the tug-boat let go of us. We put sail on her and headed for the open sea.

CHAPTER TWENTY-FOUR

AND REACTIONS

We were bound for Redondo, southern California. It was the month of January, and cold and snappy. Having possession of the sounding rod, I was in a position to encourage the crew, although they received my well-meant promptings with scornful sarcasm. They pumped, I pumped, and the captain pumped, and even the cook between intervals of cooking; we pumped, and pumped, and pumped. We did manage to keep her down to about three feet of water in the hold.

Finally there came a night when the storm-bound sun, striped with yellow streamers, crammed into the ocean. By the time the sidelights were lighted and fastened into the screens, the wind had a vicious whip to it, and the waves from out the evening shadows rushed in upon the defenceless ship like a strange army of humpy creatures.

It was interesting to the nautical eye to watch the manœuvres of the captain and the Irishman.

"Reef her down!" roared the captain, now entirely renouncing his superstitious fears for real action, as a real sailor will do every time.

" The curse of God on the day I ever rounded the

AND REACTIONS

Horn!" shouted the Irishman. "Here we are, mind yez, in a hurricane, and in an auld ship that opens up her seams to let the ocean in. It's a good mind I have not to do a hand's turn—just let her sink and drowned yez like rats!"

"You'll drown no rats on her this trip," I shouted to him for the pure mischief of it.

His raging reply was drowned by a little stubby Swede, who had also heard, and now breasted the wind and walked up to me.

"Did you say there ban no rats on her?"

"Yes," I said, "they left her this trip at Garden City."

"Oh, by Yiminy, Mike!" he shouted to the Irishman, "the rats ban gone!"

It was pitch-dark now, and the spray from the waves threw shadows of light across the deckload, but not enough to show the expression of Mike's face when the Swede told him that the rats had left the ship. There is something about an Irishman in a crisis that is different from most people. When hope is gone he doesn't want to be told about it. He may feel more the danger of dying, due perhaps to training and superstition, but to say to him, "This is the end, let us make our peace with God," would be an invitation to him to fight you before the end did come.

The news flew around among the crew. With the rising storm the situation was really serious without the added dread caused by deserting rats. Silence settled on the men, while each took stock of himself after his own fashion. No one felt the solemnity of it all more than Mike, but when the Swede spoke up, "Well, by Yiminy, this is the last of us," Mike flew at him.

"Arrah, to hell wid yez! Shure, it's wailing like a banshee ye are. What does an auld rat amount to, anyway? Shure, they left the auld hooker because they were all starved to death, that's what they did, and who would blame them? Let's reef her down, me boys, she's a foine little ship, so she is."

We reefed her down and hove her to, and all the while Mike sang songs of love and songs of hate, but never a song of fear.

The captain, feeling temporary relief from anxiety, returned to the consolation of his superstitions, and asked Mike to stop singing, thinking that his high notes caused the apexes of the wind, which seemingly did accompany them.

"It's bad enough as it is," whined the squirming captain, "without tantalizing the elements."

The wind, like the night, came stronger. The ship rolled, groaned, and flung herself carelessly at the humpy ocean. When an extra-daring sea would leap to the high deckload and find its level on the heads of the pumpers, the Swede would cry out: "Another like that ban the last of us!" Then Mike would roar:

"Keep yere clapper closed! Sure it'll be the loikes of ye that'll be driving me from the sea, and not the storms at all, at all!"

The night was gloomy, and the sight of the captain made it gloomier still. He kept running from the barometer to the pump, crying:

"Didn't I know that it would come to this!"

As he peered at the compass, the binnacle light shining in his face showed there wrinkles of tortured anxiety.

Morning came at last, with a topaz sky casting an angry glare on an agitated sea. The wind whipped and bit at the leaking ship as she shivered in the violence of the waves. The part of her hull that was not submerged would rise up to their taunts like a black-finned mammoth from the deep, writhing in torture.

Towards noon the weather grew better; we gave her more sail and headed her away on her course. For nineteen days we pumped to keep her afloat until we reached Redondo. We hardly had any sleep, and our aching muscles hardened and grew to monstrous size.

The port had neither harbour nor tug-boats, and the open sea washed in against the wharfs, running far out from the shore. When we came to anchor and the ship brought strain on the cable, it snapped. Then the long ground swells took possession of the ship and soon made a total wreck of her on the sandy beach. We threw a line out to the life-savers and scrambled ashore, each and all.

I was very happy to have my feet finally touch the sand, for I had a red-haired sweetheart in that town, and I set out to find her. She was there sure enough but with nary a spark of love in her eyes for a shipwrecked sailor. Shortly after she was married to a young Custom House inspector, and I scratched another red-haired lady from my memory.

We were paid off at Redondo, and with money in our pockets we headed for Murphy's saloon to drink one another's health. The captain and I left Mike and the Swede with their arms around each other, singing " Rolling Home across the Sea," as we started by rail for San Francisco.

The owners were glad to see us and happy that we could not bring their rotten old ship into port again. If we had gone down in her it would have been regrettable, although, after all, our risk. Still, they were pleased that we should live to pump another day. Quite a different greeting we received from the insurance company. One would have thought that we were criminals, from the gruelling they gave us. However, we stuck to the truth, try as they might to shake us, and in the end the owners received a large sum of money for their worthless, unseaworthy ship.

Since then the days of owners have changed much, as have the days of ship structure. No more the harassed, hard-headed owners, with whom a master had personal relations at least ; no more the feeling of responsibility to a person, the changing expressions of whose face you knew so well ; no more knock-down arguments, desperate efforts to please, sharp words, and hard-won praise. I have known a captain to win a suit of new sails with the gift of a conch-shell. For the captain whose heart was really in his work there was the reward in having his owner out night after night, watching for the delayed ship, sending news to the family, then giving him the rare word of praise and the bonus cheque.

When the East India Company dissolved, each employee who had served five years was given a bonus, while those who had served ten years, even the humblest, were pensioned. This, even though there had been no prior agreement with the employees, who had been both well treated and paid, and also given the opportunity to make considerable money trading.

Nowadays the shipping world has grown so large that the commanders and men of steel ships are deprived of their tacking and wearing, their little schemes and their rewards. They are no more than scheduled items on a huge pay-roll, liable to instantaneous and unexplained discharge, mechanically ordered, seldom pensioned, and almost never specially recognized, except in a routine way. The efficiency man rather than the owner gets their complaints, and personal interest is a routine affair, limited by obedience to printed orders, sobriety, and adherence to schedule.

I don't understand it very well, and I suppose to most seamen to-day the sure protection they have against bad treatment, which we didn't have in the old days, is preferable. Nevertheless, I am glad I was a sailing-ship man.

CHAPTER TWENTY-FIVE

SALMON FISHING

Some months after I took the hare-lipped captain's schooner to port, I found myself on the Fraser River, British Columbia. It was summer, the salmon season was on, and with a boat and net from a cannery, I went gill-netting for salmon.

A young man who had a wife and child living in New Westminster was my boat-puller. He was a steady, hard-working man. It was towards the close of the salmon run, and we were thinking of giving up fishing. It would hardly pay to continue because of the physical wear and tear, for the few salmon there were in the river. Yet he prevailed on me to fish for another week, and I consented.

That Sunday afternoon before we put out to fish I took a nap, and when I awoke I was somewhat troubled. I had dreamed that I saw my dead self being lowered into a grave at home in Ireland, and I was amused, as I stood there by the grave, watching the mourners cover my dead self up. They used no earth to cover the coffin, but each one had a pail, and in each pail was water, and this they poured into the open grave. When it was full to the top, the water-carriers disappeared.

SALMON FISHING

I told my dream to my boatman. He enjoyed the story, and we had a good laugh at the idea of me in a watered grave.

"Come on," said he then, "let's go down and get the net off the rack and into the boat. When that's done, it will be time to go out and fish."

In British Columbia the law was that there should be no nets in the water from sunrise Saturday until sunset Sunday evening. When we were ready we hoisted the sail and put out into the gulf. As the sun went down I cast the net, intending as usual to drift all night, pick it up in the morning light, and sail with the salmon home to market.

This night it was different. With the afterglow of the sun came black clouds, and the night set in like a monstrous shadow, shutting out all but the aurorean gleam from the lighthouse. Unushered, the wind came in stormy gusts and lashed the sea to rage. That night was the last for seventy-two fishermen. Thirty-six seaworthy boats went down like cockle-shells before its hungry onslaught.

I gathered the net aboard, hoping to make Stevestown at the mouth of the Fraser River before the worst of the storm should overtake us. Even before I could pull in the net I had trouble to keep the boat from turning over. She was a large fishing craft, twenty-four feet over all, with a six-foot beam, a round bottom, and bowed at both ends. Yet that night she had the motion of a light canoe adrift in a waterfall.

I put the mast up and tied two reefs in the sail.

Catching a glimmer from the lighthouse, I shaped a course for the river. There were dangers, I knew, in crossing the shallow bars with the sea running wild. If I should strike one, I knew that nothing could save me.

My dream of the afternoon came back to me vividly, but I crowded it away, for it was my intention to fight the wind and waves in spite of their sudden attack. I ground my teeth and grabbed the tiller, eased the sheet, and we were away—either to safety or death.

I called to my boat-puller to get forward to the bow, and keep a sharp look-out to avoid running into other fishermen. The wind and waves fairly lifted the boat out of the water—we made such speed. I could scarcely see a finger before my eyes. The danger of allowing the boat to broach the sea was as great as striking a sandbar. Between the two dangers, and with my dream ever pushing into my mind, I sailed on.

Half an hour later I heard screams; many there were, screams from drowning lost men: Japanese calling on Buddha, Indians invoking their Spirits, white men imploring their God. All, all, crying for Life and strangling in the cruel snare of Death!

To sail on amidst capsized fishing boats was playing quoits with fate. Realizing this new danger, I called out to my boat-puller to look out for himself. I determined to come up into the wind and sea. My best chance lay in the open sea. If not there—well, one more fishing boat would be lost.

SALMON FISHING

I hauled in the sheet and put the tiller over. Like a race-horse she rounded into the waves, swamped herself full to the gunwales, but did not, as I expected, turn bottom up. I called to the boat-puller: "Throw the anchor overboard!" I got no response.

Fearing the worst—that he had been pitched into the sea—I repeated the order again. No response. Then I realized that I was alone, and my heart began to pound. I thought that I too was doomed. If only I could manage to get forward and get the anchor out she would swing head on to the storm. This would help to prolong the end, for we carried a sea anchor with seventy-five feet of rope.

The water in the boat was nigh up to my waist. I wallowed through it and got out the anchor. Then I heaved the net overboard, bailed the water out, and she swung bow on to the waves with the strain on the anchor rope. I bailed, while the storm roared unceasingly, until daybreak.

The morning brought sun and calming waves. The wind took flight to some distant sea, and I gave thanks for another day. The bloated bodies of seventy-two fishermen beached on the sands. I hunted for my puller, found him, and took the body to the wife who loved him, and to the child who chattered and smiled in the face of Death. I had made some money fishing that I did not need. This I gave to the widow and went on my way—which was much the way of the winds.

CHAPTER TWENTY-SIX

THE REVIVAL OF LIDA

WHEN I first left the sea I went to mining. The gold rivers of Alaska drew me, the craggy Andes, and the desert plains of Australia. Finally I drifted to Goldfield, Nevada. That was in 1903. There was a boom on then and a few of the mines held high-grade ore. Ten thousand people were out to get it. The camp was wide open: nothing barred. Justifiable homicide was the verdict for those who were quick with the trigger, and it behoved the tenderfoot to get acclimatized with the utmost speed to those who sniffed the alkali. There was no room for friendliness in that great selfish clamour. Everyone was digging for himself.

The mountains that had hitherto guarded their secrets from the lust of men were now assailed, gouged, and cut, exposing their treasure in a few places. Burros and pack-mules climbed the steep trails, their new masters pushing, and cursing, and clubbing them along. Like hungry locusts, these men, of no particular nationality and little love of home, swept the hills as if to raven on the bushes and the dust.

Like the drift from a wreck, I too was swept

along by a comber of greed, to join in the conquest of cañon and peak. I bought burros, bacon, beans, and flour, picks and shovels and drilling steels. I rambled the hills and gophered holes. I staked claims and located towns and water sites. I foresaw myself a large financier, and talked in millions, as did everyone else there. I wandered in time to Lida, not far from Goldfield.

Lida had been an old silver camp, and in the early 'sixties a booming town. This much was told me by an old squaw man who lived there. He was one of those old miners who stayed on in a town after the mines were played out, in the hope that some day it would awake once more to the click of the pistol and the bray of the burro.

He was an Austrian by birth, and his name ended in " vitch." I could never pronounce it. With him lived a squaw, whose face was furrowed with desert wrinkles like kinks in a juniper. He treated her much as he would an outlaw cayuse, kicking and beating her when he felt like it, until prosperity made him independent of the little comfort she gave him. Then one day she died suddenly, with all the symptoms of poisoning. It was said that he had doped a bottle of whisky for her. There was no law to punish him, so he buried her alongside the pump in the backyard. Once covered up, she was soon forgotten. In spite of all this, he had a kind of pathetic appeal to him, so that when he told a story to the miners about his poor old mother in Austria, they swallowed it, and his drinks too.

But I am straying ahead of my story. When I first saw him the squaw was alive, and he and she lived in a 'dobe house at the head of what had once been the principal street of Lida. The sage brush was growing over it then, covering the wagon ruts, and up on the hill beyond was the graveyard, shrouded in underbrush, dead as dead could be. Few if any of the miners buried there had died natural deaths, as the scrawly hand-written grave-boards bore witness.

Still, no decay could wholly obliterate the memories of former greatness, and it was decreed that Lida should come to life again after forty years. A new generation of miners arrived and began to dig where the old generation had left off. The town site was grubbed, the brush burned up, and lots were sold to new-comers. Tents went up, and the squaw man started a saloon. Chips rattled and pistols clicked. Lida was herself again.

The Austrian's dream had come true. He owned the town site, and money came in fast. His only trouble was with an occasional "lot jumper"—someone who was rash enough to settle in dispute of his quit-claim title to the town lots. But this trouble was a small item, being quickly settled with a gun. He was a big man now and dictated the policies of the tent town, and signed as many cheques as he cashed.

One day, when the old town had been new about six months, a stranger drove up in an automobile. There was nothing unusual in this, but there was something unusual in the man. Big and broad and strong he looked, and his round face showed good feeding. The tan of the desert was missing. His eyes were black and penetrating, and he gave out an air of confidence and power. His tight lips concealed a mouth well filled with fine teeth and covered by a jet-black moustache. He must have been past middle age, for his hair was greying at the temples. He threw off his linen duster with a superior swagger.

"Yes," said he, without preliminary, his compelling eye roving over a chance group of miners as he strode about, limbering his legs. "Yes, boys, I'm going to do things here that will astonish the natives. I'm going to put Lida on the map."

"Vot's dot?" asked the Austrian, sidling up to him with elbows squared. "Vot's dot?"

The stranger saw fit to dispose of him with a stare which had been useful on other similar occasions. The Austrian growled and backed away.

That night there was a meeting in Dutch John's saloon. The stranger took charge. He bought the miners drinks and told them of Lida's wonderful possibilities. At first, when their vision had been unclouded, they had been inclined to think him an unscrupulous promoter and crook. Now they fell for his golden words.

"Right at your door, gentlemen," he cried in concluding a flowery and powerful speech, "under your eyes, beneath these grand old peaks, is one of the richest gold camps in the world. It is no more than right that we should dedicate a city of granite blocks to those noble spires that have been true to their trust these million years, even if, as my engineers tell me, it will be necessary to abandon the present town site for one on the slope of the hill. Near here, Men of the Hills, are the graves of silent pioneers. If each of those mouldering forms could rise up and speak to you, I am sure they would say, 'Move and buy, and be not afraid, for the future is golden.'"

Then he bought drinks and shook each miner by the hand. As he searched the faces, his black eyes spoke: "I'm here to trim you, and trim you to my liking."

It was plain that the stranger had them, and the squaw man told them so. He reduced the price of his lots—a quarter—a half—and then he had the main street ploughed and rolled, while they commented on how much better it looked. He too gave the miners free drinks. His corral gate was opened, and the town burros he-hawed in, and nibbled at the baled hay. The burro men were pleased, and slapped the squaw man on the back, assuring him of their loyalty to the old town.

At last he gave way to his emotion. With his old face warped in coyote grins he cried: "Vel, boys, I haf von ting to do before I vos dead."

The burro men looked at each other. The squaw man waved them away as they tried to pat him on the back. He was shaking as if with a chill. The flimsy pine bar shook with him and the glasses rattled. Again he spoke: "I do it, and I do it queek!"

He got no further, for a shadow broke the desert light on the floor, and the stranger stood in the doorway.

"Give us a drink, Dutchy," he said quietly, as if the very atmosphere were not charged with hate of him, and as quietly he moved up to the bar.

The old desert-bleached hand of the squaw man reached under the bar and brought up a revolver. The burro men scattered like scud before a gale, but the stranger stood there leaning against the bar, looking quietly into the terrible face of Dutchy.

Licking his dry lips, Dutchy spoke: "I vos going to kill you, you damned crook. You steal my town up mit de hill."

The piercing black eyes of the stranger covered those of Dutchy, as he walked along the bar without a word and wrenched the revolver from him, easily, deliberately. Then he slapped him on the jaw.

"Dutchy," he said, and the miners outside the door began to come back at the words, "you can poison squaws, and shoot men in the back, but when it comes to an even break you are a coward. Now hurry and get drinks for the boys. Come on in," he called, "the fight is over, and Dutchy feels better now."

We drank, and the stranger pulled out a great roll of bills, stripping them down until he came to a twenty, on which Dutchy's eyes fastened with the look of a greedy hound. The stranger bade him keep the change.

The stranger's reputation was made now. He had proven his steel to the natives of Lida. He was one of those great men of pioneer times whose genius was real, no matter how misdirected. He was an old hand at the game of fleecing, and he knew that before you commence to shear the sheep, you must first get them corralled.

He slung his money about like a drunken sailor, and everyone, even the Piute Indians, sung his praises. We believed that there was fabulous wealth in the hills, and that his purpose was to build comfortable homes for the men of the desert, as he said, " to help put windows into the mountains," that we might see the fortunes which were to be ours for the asking.

When a man of the stranger's type visits a desert mining town it is not from choice, but to create a gap in the trail of his reputation. Unfortunately he, who could have played high finance equally well on the square, had chosen the line of least resistance in hidden places.

He had a record, which included a penitentiary term. It was said that he had sold the warden fifteen thousand dollars worth of wild-cat stock, and yet secured a pardon. He had been a lawyer, and was gifted with a mind that could squeeze him out of any tight place. His scheme for the new town site in Lida was backed by a Goldfield bank that had no scruples about spending depositors' money. So the new town site was cleared of sage brush, streets were laid out, and sites pegged out.

In vain the squaw man offered us inducements to stay. His cowardice and greed had killed his further chances in the face of the stranger's liberality and promises, and like the sheep again, we rolled up our tents and moved them up the hill to the new town.

By this time the stranger had six automobiles, all new, running from Goldfield and bringing in newcomers with money to buy lots. A one-plank sidewalk was laid, which was only a preliminary to the granite buildings, but it inspired confidence, for lumber was one hundred and fifty dollars a thousand feet at the railroad sixty miles away. It cost three cents a pound to haul it to Lida by mule team.

The stranger cared nothing for these minor matters of expense. The bank in Goldfield had plenty of money. The sap-headed depositors were too busy in the mountains hunting gold to bother their heads about banks or plank sidewalks.

CHAPTER TWENTY-SEVEN

A DAY OF RECKONING

DUTCHY was alone now. No inducement he could offer would hold anyone, and he was left to himself and the company of stray burros, and the dead squaw under the pump. His hair and beard grew long and weedy; his finger-nails looked like the talons of an eagle; his overalls and shirt-front were spattered with flour dough. He refused to visit the new town, although the stranger, knowing that he had money, used every wile to get him there. He stayed on in old Lida, praying for vengeance.

The mountains chimed the echo of pounding steel. The exploding giant powder rang through the cañons like the roar of an angry bull. Hillsides were torn open by the hungry, gaunt, and ravenous miners. Women were there too, with boots and picks on their shoulders, and as savage in their scrambling greed as the male "desert rats."

The old graveyard of the 'sixties was grubbed of its underbrush, and a fence put around it. Many fresh graves were made for the men who were clumsy with a gun. When a man died, very little attention was paid to him. He was boxed up as a matter of course, dumped into the grave, and as quickly forgotten. There was a doctor, but he had waited until he was forty-five to graduate from a correspondence course. Meantime he ran a hoist——

If that doctor had understood his business he could have saved the life of a woman who had given much and received little but whisky, grunts, and kicks from the men of Lida. She was just an ordinary prostitute, but when she lay stretched in death on a cot in the back end of a saloon, those rough men of the hills threw down their picks and put their giant powder away, and wandered solemnly into town. They were going to give her a funeral, so they sent for a Scotchman back in the hills, who in days gone by had been a Presbyterian minister.

Meanwhile another sorrow was on the wing to Lida, far greater to the minds of most men than the death of her who had bartered her body that brutes might satisfy their lust—then scorn her.

The bank in Goldfield, to which the stranger had given his brains so that the new town of Lida should grow, now had about all the people's money that it needed. The president and the cashier accordingly absconded, stealing everything but a five-dollar gold piece and a five-cent piece that rolled under the safe. This was all that was left of a hundred thousand dollars of deposits. The news was to strike Lida when the miners were in from the hills, drawn by the funeral to meet in a greater grief.

They were all small depositors, and their hundred dollars or so represented years of deprivation in the desert: misery, thirst, and hunger. Lida would be swept off the map as quickly as she had been put on it. Her granite buildings, that were to welcome the morning rays of the desert sun, must now mirage the spectre of a thief's glory—the granite ghost of yesterday.

That day the stranger did not turn his keen black conquering eyes towards Lida. By the time the stage-coach heralded the disaster, he had sought trails still more hidden from the light of day. The driver of the stage-coach owned lots in Lida, and was a depositor in the Goldfield bank. He whipped his horses most of the thirty miles to get to Lida. The news settled on the town like the March wind that brings hail.

A raw and restless quiver was in the air. Men were not to be trifled with that day. A double duty called them. They had not forgotten their reverence for the open grave, but their eyes shifted quickly away to where the sky and sage met—where some puff of dust might betray a fugitive bank robber.

The ex-preacher arrived late in the afternoon. He was tired, and so was the cayuse he rode. He was a heavy man, fat from eating sow's belly and beans. His cheeks were flabby and hairy, his knuckles were skinned, and the loose soles on his worn-out boots flopped when he walked. His khaki trousers had been whipped clean by the brush as he squeezed through. The men of Lida had been waiting for him since the stage-coach came in. That had been two long hours ago—years of suspense they seemed.

A man of the desert, whose casual eye is his companion in danger, might have sensed the preparations for a skirmish. Horses, saddled and bridled, pranced nervously, snapping at the halters that bound them to tent-pegs. Wild-looking bronchos, hitched to buckboards, reared back in their harness, then plunged forward, anxious to get away. The miners were armed with notched rifles and revolvers, some with light-hearted mother-of-pearl adornment to make their work more palatable, yet the expression on their faces outdid the threat of their weapons, so grim they were, so resolute in restraint, so death-respecting, and death-dealing.

The preacher went to the saloon where the body of the dead woman lay. "Give me some beer," he demanded, and they gave him beer. "Now we'll take up the corpse," he announced, "and go to the graveyard and bury it."

It was a quarter of a mile up the hill to the grave. There the body of the woman was tenderly carried on the shoulders of men who were quick on their feet and quick with their eyes. She might have been a precious gem, such delicate care was given to the lowering of the body into the open hole. Hats were off. The preacher stood on the mound of loose dirt that was soon to cover her. The serenity of peace seemed to descend on the miners. The hill and the cañon below were in shadow, and beyond the peaks of the Panamint were ablaze in amber colouring. What a strange event! Half a thousand men with heads bared, bowed over the grave of a whore! Half a thousand ruined men, waiting to be released for revenge!

The preacher read a burial service and spoke a simple word in defence of the faults that had been the ruin of her. Then he called on them to sing, "Nearer, my God, to Thee," leading the hymn in a rich baritone. One by one those soul-hardened men joined in, and as they sang their faces relaxed, softening the lines of labour, and greed, hatred and anguish.

As they finished there was a great clearing of throats. The preacher, looking down on the grave, solemnly said: "Let us all offer a silent prayer, that her soul may take wing from these cañons and ranges, and on to the East where the dark clouds grow less, on to the King Star whose brilliant aurora will cleanse it and cure it from Earth's wandering wounds."

The heads were bent again, and as the prayer went out, an uncanny silence crept over the grave, a silence that the sea creates, broken sometimes by the leap of a fish or the spout of a whale.

This silence was broken by a laugh—a laugh that had the ring of hate, lust, selfish greed, and madness —and a muddled articulation of oaths and groans

A DAY OF RECKONING

and epithets. Somewhere in the crowd a rifle spoke, and less than a quarter of a mile away the squaw man dropped into the brush to laugh no more. The ex-preacher raised his head and shouted "Amen."

They filled in the grave and tamped the loose soil around, so that the coyotes might not burrow in and disturb her. The job was done without haste. As the night shadows gathered from the hills the miners walked away, not in the solemn way they had come, but with a quick, freed step which led them to their saddle-horses and buckboards.

Like a charge of cavalry they were off; dust dashed into the darkness. The bank robbers had a twelve hours' start, but two days later the president and the cashier were caught.

They were not killed, but brought back and made to stand trial. Nevada had no banking laws then. All that was required was a sign on the door: "Bank open from ten till three." Depositors had no protection. The trial, which was paid for with stolen money, was put off from time to time, and eventually thrown out of court.

The stranger had disappeared before the crash came, but soon afterwards he was heard from again. A desert editor, the newspaper said, had blown off his head with a sawed-off shot-gun.

Lida was no more. Jackrabbits ran unhindered where the town had stood. The sage brush began to grow over new and old graves alike. The hills lay pock-marked, pitted. The microbe, man, had gone somewhere to bore another hole. Time, with its charter of shifting sands, would fill the pits, and the afterglow of the early 'sixties would haze the hills in ether waves, and cover the spots with sage and shist.

The money-and-faith-robbed miners, I among them, scattered to new work. It was in Goldfield, shortly afterwards, that typhoid fever overtook me.

My doctor, who loved to needle himself with morphine, told me afterwards that I had had a narrow escape, and I believed him, judging from the trouble I had to learn to walk again. The Goldfield undertakers, too, had been making inquiries about me, as to where I lived, and whether I had much money. They throve there in those days: five hundred dollars for a pine box! If the bereaved lived outside the state, and wanted the body, the lead casing around the coffin cost the price of a desert convoy.

At this time the wife I had married when I was captain of a coastwise ship on the Pacific coast, left me. A squall from the desert arose from the cactus and sage brush and blew us apart. What money I had saved from the wreck in Lida went to pay doctor, druggist, and hospital. I had rheumatism, and limped around on a couple of canes. My longing for the sea came back with insistent urging; I wanted to raise enough money to go back.

One of Tiffany's engineers examined a turquoise

claim that I held and approved it. Tiffany offered to buy on a bond sale, with a cash payment down of five thousand dollars. I was happy again, but not for long. Another crook crossed my trail with falsified affidavits of previous ownership. That meant endless litigation. Tiffany was not buying a lawsuit, and my deal fell through.

I hobbled away to another camp, where I met the young man I had helped in Vancouver. He now assisted me back to strength, and sent me away with money in my pocket. I went straight to San Francisco and feasted on Dungeness crabs the night of my arrival. That night I felt the comfort of clean linen sheets, so different from the dirty, dusty sage tuck blankets of the desert. With the sigh that brings relaxation, like that of a child after a hard cry, I fell asleep, to dream of gold-mines in Ireland.

I was suddenly awakened, about five in the morning. The walls came tumbling down upon me, and I thought I'd choke with lime dust.

The door leading to the stairs was warped and I could not open it. For a moment a prayer for deliverance flashed through my mind, then the sailor in me rebelled at resignation and took command. I fished a chair out of a pile of bricks and drove it through the door.

Out in the street that morning I dressed, with thousands of other people whose lives had been miraculously spared. I could disregard the loss of all my papers, and the treasured, useless, invaluable souvenirs of a lifetime, as I helped, during those three days of agonized suffering, with the rescue work. Then I booked passage by steamer to Puget Sound.

CHAPTER TWENTY-EIGHT

SALE MAKING

A NIGHT or two later, in Tacoma, I was sitting in an hotel lobby, wondering what to do next. A large flabby man, with intelligent kindly eyes, squeezed himself into the chair alongside of me. We talked of the weather, of the people going past outside the window, and of the thousands who had suffered in the earthquake. Then he encouraged me to talk of myself, and I sketched my life for him in some detail: not cheerfully, I must admit.

He listened with interest, for he seemed to fancy me. When I had done he said : " What's the loss of a few dollars ? " Unbuttoning his coat, he exposed a large morocco-bound book, in his inner pocket. " It amounts to nothing. Why, you haven't found yourself yet, that's the trouble. I was forty years old before I found myself, and the result is that last year I made twenty thousand dollars, and this year promises to double that amount."

He talked on, fairly bristling with energy. Then he leaned towards me.

" It's seldom that I do what I am going to do for you," he whispered. " I am going to take you along with me and show you how to pile up money."

"Doing what?" I asked. I'll grant him that he had me swamped with the thought of dollars, and I felt as nervous as a bank robber.

He pulled the morocco-bound book from his pocket. His eyes shone with enthusiasm; he forgot that we were not alone in the hotel. He slapped the book down on the arm of the chair and shouted:

"This is what we get our money from! The *Students' Reference*, in three volumes, sold in every home in the U.S. for nineteen dollars and seventy-five cents! Children knock you down in the street for it! Women weep for the privilege of buying it from you! Five dollars commission on each set, and ten sets you sell every day! Four hours' work! Three hundred dollars a week! Friends by the thousands! Crazy about you! Too many! A wonderful business!"

Giving me no time even to catch my breath, he jumped to his feet, and telling me to meet him next morning at nine o'clock, he trotted rapidly off to the elevator. As it whisked him out of sight, he called back a final "Good night!"

Two hours later, the hotel being cleared of the litter of the day, and the yawning clerks and the busy night porter willing me off to bed, I went. My mind was still foggy, as it had been for the past two hours, with books and greenbacks, and the hope of regaining ease and self-respect.

I met the book man at nine o'clock the following

SALE MAKING

morning. He had lost none of the charm of the night before. We flew to talking, and I went to work under his instructions, selling books.

For three months I was a successful book agent, making money easily. My line of argument was simple enough. I would go into a saloon, for instance, and finding it run by an Italian, I would ask him if he could tell me when Garibaldi was born. No? Well, how did he expect to answer arguments that started over the bar? Look here, I would show him. Here on page 113 was a full account of Garibaldi. This book would answer any question that came up, and even settle a fight. He ought to keep it in the safe. It would be as valuable to him as all the money he had there. His children were going to school. They could get help from this book to supplement their studies and send them up the ladder to higher learning.

And to the village school teacher I would say: " You simply can't afford not to have this book by your elbow. What are you going to do when the children ask questions and you can't answer them, and they go home and tell their fathers and mothers that teacher doesn't know? You are entrusted with the care of unfolding and inquiring minds, and if you are to be true to the trust these people put in you, you will not leave a page of this book unturned, but produce its invaluable information every chance you have, thereby proving your own superior intelligence."

But as if some fluency lay in money so easily

gained, it went as if it had no value, and seemed to lack the power to accumulate. The superstition of a sailor told me there was no good in money ill gained. By what right, I reasoned, did I assume control of my fellow-beings to the extent that I was imposing something on them that they did not really want, for which they must deprive themselves materially? How could I deny responsibility, shrugging it on to them for being so easily dominated? It seemed to be a kind of black art I was practising. God forbid, I thought, and gave it up.

As I look back on it now, I still can see it no other way, for the rich and poor alike were helpless in our hands. Our arguments flowed over them, covered them, swamped them, sucked them under—and they were gone, as if their money were ours, not theirs.

So I went back to the sea again, to clean soiled hands with Stockholm tar.

CHAPTER TWENTY-NINE

FAREWELLS

One day, shortly after I had left the book business, I was in a small town on Puget Sound looking for a ship. Strolling around, I was attracted by a crowd in front of a general store. Policemen were running and women screaming, and with one thing and another there seemed to be no end of excitement.

Always being of a curious nature, I hurried with the rest to the store, elbowing my way through the crowd as I went, in order not to miss the finish, whatever it might be. As I wriggled through the outer straggling edge and made my way to the hushed circle around a clearing on the sidewalk, I saw a tall, lank policeman stretched out there bleeding. Standing over him, triumphant, making no effort to get away, and as drunk as drunk could be, stood none other than Liverpool Jack.

He was bareheaded, his coat was off, and his shirt was torn to ribbons. His hairy bare arms exposed to curious gaze their tattooed ladies, ships, anchors, and flags of many nations. For a moment I felt the distance I had travelled mentally and materially since Jack and I had been mates. I was no better than I had been, but whether it was a feeling of difference caused by having had money, or whether some real refinement had grown out of what I had known at home—anyway, I shrank at the sight of him. Then my loyalty shamed me, and I became alert to help him out.

Fortunately I did not have a chance to speak to him then, for three strapping policemen, well armed, grabbed hold of him, and putting the "twisters" on his wrists, led him to the lock-up. Jack did not see me and I did not want him to, until I should have time to find the best way to come to his aid.

While the crowd helped the policeman to his feet, the man who owned the general store told me about the fight. It seems that the "cop" had imprudently undertaken to arrest Liverpool Jack single-handed, when he came upon him, drunk in the street. The cop was promptly thrown through the window of the general store, where Jack's follow-up work did all possible damage to a loose display of potatoes, apples, cereals, and tobacco.

The store-keeper was mourning his loss and damning the inefficient policeman. Who was to pay him for his goods? he whined. Who, indeed? Speeding away to the jail, I managed to secure Jack's release by paying a two-hundred-dollar fine. Before the poor store-keeper had time to figure up his damage, we were out of town and on our way to Tacoma.

There we had to wait a few days for a ship.

FAREWELLS

To be sure of his safety, I was now going to take him to sea with me. But one night he slipped away, and I never again saw him alive. Next day his body was found on the railroad track, mutilated by a train. I went to a saloon where Jack was known. They told me there that he had said since there was no one to fight with any more he guessed he might as well pull a few trains off the track.

This statement may not have been true, but it was characteristic of the man the poor dead creature had been. Even in death he seemed not to have found peace: there was a savage set to his jaw. I must remember him as he looked then, and feel sorry that the terrible scrappiness had been the end of him, and not the real tender-heartedness that I knew lay beneath. Poor, poor, lonesome Liverpool Jack!

With the last of my book-agent money I had him buried. I hope that the better part of him has found a release and is going on, sailing oceans, splicing ropes, and tattooing other souls of fighting children of the sea.

For two years now I rambled the oceans as mate, and sometimes master of fine ships almost of my choice—for I was seasoned and knew something of men, and was free of that which in my youth had made me unreliable.

Yet the sea, however much she may still the thirst for change, is no husbander of men's strength against the future. I realized this at last, perhaps because youth was gone, even to Liverpool Jack, who had been the connecting-link, and I turned my thoughts landward again.

The slow saving of a seaman's wages was a process untried by me ever, and my conception of provision for the future was a gold-mine. Gold in the hills, waiting somewhere for me. Somewhere opportunity for rest, and a home. As I set out on my quest, more and more my thoughts returned to Ireland. I longed to go back with even a little stake, to see my mother, to buy a little piece of land near her, to have my dog and my horse, my chickens and my pigs, and perhaps some day—when the past should have buried its dead—some day a son of my own to raise, fearless of me and of the world. . . .

Thoughts of home were ever bound up in my mother, and although I knew well enough that if I had not been stubbornly foolish I could have been back in Ireland this many a year, prosperous, and a delight to her, yet it never occurred to me that there might not be plenty of time—that she might be nearing the end of her span.

So the news that she was dead found me digging, and gold turned hard and lifeless before my eyes, while Love sat there beside me, bleeding. Blinded by sorrow I went a-roving, and the steep braes knew me. I picked and dug and washed from habit, for good luck meant only food to me now. Often there was no food, nor even water for that matter, although when thirst gets you,

you cannot will to die, however cheaply you may hold your life.

And so six years went by, the loneliness of the mountains healing me, and I was a better man.

CHAPTER THIRTY

THE OLD MAN OF THE VIOLET ROCK

It was at a time when I was mining, where the Snake River makes a boundary line between Idaho and Oregon. From seventy miles away came the report of a big gold strike. I lost no time in getting there, but the report proved a fluke, based on a prospector's finding of a sparse outcropping of gold.

I left the place as quickly as I had come. This time I took a trail that led me about a hundred miles away from the railroad, into a country where there was no mining, and little of anything but barren waste land. Why my impulse took me there I cannot say.

My new trail led me towards a long and crooked river—the Owyhee. It ploughs through deep gorges, and again expands quietly where the cañons widen out. Along its banks green patches spread themselves fertilely, like oases in the desert. It was on one of these green stretches that I met the Old Man of Violet Rock.

I had been travelling all day long without seeing a human being. I was hungry, and my horse was tired. On the western side of the river a huge mountain lay hooded in mourning, snugly capped

OLD MAN OF THE VIOLET ROCK

with lava; the evening sun perched on top. I was riding along the eastern bank, at the foot of a perpendicular sandstone precipice of a thousand feet or more, from which a steep tableland had broken off. Here were caves, semicircular, many of them quite large, from which issued a peculiar odour. Wild animals probably carried their plunder into them to appease their hunger in peace, or perhaps within was taking place the decomposition of an ancient race.

The sun had rolled over and down behind the lava cap now. As I rode on, my horse was startled by a squeaky, groaning sound. I dismounted, and leading him, walked ahead. It was not more than three hundred yards to the river, yet I dreaded even this short walk, for it was the month of July and rattlesnakes challenged me as I wended my way through the sage brush towards the groaning sound. There at the edge of the river was an old water-wheel, run by the current and labouring furiously, with a groan and a squeak, but lifting the water nevertheless to a flume. My horse neighed, and I felt relieved. We both knew that not far from that water-wheel must be some sort of a home where we could rest and feed.

Following the water ditch a quarter of a mile, I came to a lava rock. Anyone would have stopped to admire it, so unusual it was, large, isolated, lying there on the bank of the river. A net-wire fence stood around three sides, and the fourth side faced the river. It would have been difficult for anyone to reach it from that side, where the drop to the water was a sheer twenty feet.

While my horse nibbled at a bunch of withered grass, I leaned against the fence and looked in. There must have been half an acre in the enclosure—the rock took up one-third of that. It stood high, peaked and irregular, with a broad base. From its summit one could command a far view up and down the river. What attracted me most was the quantity of flowers growing around and over it, startlingly colourful in the dusk—a lovely deep blue. Violets in bunches, in sods, in masses, over the rock and down its sides, in fissures somehow filled with soil, and glorying in release from desert barrenness. A neat little grassy path led over the top of the rock. I cannot quite convey the feeling of sentiment that this sight stirred in me. It was something akin to infinite peace.

While I lingered, trying to trace some reason for this blooming memorial to geological ages, an old man mounted the rock from the other side and came along the violet-strewn path towards me.

"Good evening, sir," said I, instinctively taking off my hat to the bent and venerable figure. He stood arrested, gazing intently at me with eyes the piercing quality of which was as yet untouched by time. His shoulders were stooped like the slant of a tree that has grown always away from some hard prevailing wind.

"Good evening," he replied, in a voice whose tonelessness betokened one who had talked but little with his fellow-men. As he stood there, white hair blowing in the evening breeze, he looked back at me without surprise or interest.

"If you want food and rest overnight," he said, pointing to a little-used trail along the river bank, "follow the irrigation ditch down a hundred yards. Then take the path to the left till you come to the barn, feed your horse, and come back here for your supper."

I thanked him and followed his directions. The barn was small and shut in by leafy mulberry trees. I fed the horse, and being hungry, hurried back. The old man was standing inside the fence by the rock. He held a pan in his hand, and at my approach handed it to me over the fence, saying:

"Help yourself to what you want. Then wash the pan and leave it. Here is coffee too," and he handed me a cup of real china, strangely out of keeping with the desert feast of beans and pork and biscuit in the rough pan. Seeing my thought in my face, he said quite simply, "Yes, I prefer a cup for coffee," and left me to my own conclusions.

He went to the corner of the fence and looked down the river. So great was his dignity that I should not have thought of questioning him, but I could not help wondering at his choosing to bring warm food to this apparently solid rock. He had not carried the pan far. He must have a fire and a house somewhere. But where? Evidently not inside the rock, and nowhere else visible.

As if to put a stop to my thoughts he turned back and began to question me. "Why did you come this way?" he asked.

I told him that I had not the slightest idea where I was going; that I simply wanted to ramble.

"How would you like to work for me a week or two?"

"What doing?" I asked, munching the beans.

"I have some hay to be cut and stacked, and there's work to be done on the water-wheel."

"All right," said I. "I'll do it. How about the pay?"

"I'll pay you whatever is right," said he, glancing around towards the rock suspiciously.

There was no more said about pay, nor did I doubt his good faith. I finished eating and washed the pan, handing it back to him across the fence.

"What a wonderful place for a house, there in the rock," said I tentatively.

He turned towards me savagely, his white bushy beard rearing out from his chin aggressively.

"You sleep in the barn," he cried. "You do work for me. You can't come inside this fence. Good night!"

He went around the rock, and whether away by the other side, or into the rock itself, I had no means of telling. Nor did I find out for many days, so secret was he about his movements.

What did he have in the rock to guard so carefully that he would not even let me inside the fence? I pondered as I found my way to the barn. Could

OLD MAN OF THE VIOLET ROCK

it be that in his rambles through the hills he had found gold? He seemed sane enough, and yet his eyes had that odd fiery glow of a miser, or a fanatic.

Common-sense thoughts would not set me at ease. I seemed impelled to let loose my wildest imaginings about the Old Man and the Rock. I was not afraid, and yet there was a strangeness about the whole place, rock, violets, and the man himself, that made me sleepless where I lay in my blanket in the hay. The slightest sound startled me: the stamp of a horse brought me to my feet, the rustling of the mulberry leaves sent a shiver through me, and during that night, and the nights that followed, I seemed haunted by the spirits of the strange things about me.

I must have been in the barn about four hours that first night when the noise of a falling tree scared me almost senseless. Surely there wasn't enough wind to blow it down! As I listened, trying to quiet my heart, there came to my ears the sound of the groaning water-wheel, labouring night as well as day in the current of the river.

Fearfully I opened the barn door and walked out and around the building. Then as if to give myself courage I shouted:

"What the devil's going on round here?"

Instantly there came back an answering sound:

"Ka-plunk! Ka-plunk! Ka-plunk!"

Reassured, I laughed aloud, went into the barn, slammed the door, and crawled into the saddle blanket, but not before I had cursed the beavers of the Owyhee River.

When I walked out of the barn the next morning the sun was up, but the rays had not yet reached the cañon. The old man was out on the rock, watering his violets. He might have been some strange being up there, sucking nectar from the purple glow. Indeed, he did look like a creature of the wilds. His short gnarly legs, his withered arms, suggested the limbs of a vine. He might have been a dryad. As I watched him, he picked a handful of violets and disappeared over the rock. Who could the violets be for? Did he have a wife? Again my thoughts ran rampant, worse than the night before. Curiosity, making the adventure worth while, would eventually find the secret of the violet rock.

I had breakfast from over the fence that morning, and for ten mornings after. Biscuits, bacon, or salt pork and beans, and black coffee, was the fare. I cut the hay, nine acres in all. The old Buckeye mowing machine was as ragged and worn as its owner. The sickle had to be filed many times a day. The horses were as strange as their abiding-place. They would work steadily for a while, then refuse to work entirely, fall to eating, and lie down all harnessed in the tall alfalfa. I would content myself sitting atop of the old mower, whistling till they were ready to work again; then, without warning, with a simultaneous lunge, they would be up and off, with me hard put to hold them.

The old man would not allow me to carry a whip. The horses were old, he said; they had been with him many years and no one must be unkind to them.

So it took three days to mow the hay, and I had ample time for amusement between times. There was real enjoyment in killing rattlesnakes. I carried a pitchfork for those that the sickle missed. It seemed that wherever I turned I saw or heard a rattler. To say that I was not afraid would not be telling the truth; I was as nervous and shifty as a squirrel.

In the evenings I tried to induce the old man to talk about himself, but he evaded conversation of any kind. He moved away from the rock seldom, and never when I was around.

At the end of the tenth day I was as far from knowing anything about him as I had been at the end of the first.

One afternoon when I had about finished stacking the hay, a thunderstorm came up the river, bringing rain and lightning. The noise of the thunder in the cañon was deafening. I hurried to the barn for shelter. Before I reached it the lightning struck the lava-topped mountain, loosening great boulders, which came plunging down into the river. No snake would have had time to strike me before I gained the barn. My snorting horse and I found reassurance with each other, and agreed that Violet Rock was no happy place for us.

The storm increased. It was not past three o'clock, yet night seemed to be setting in. I felt danger around me, and the sailor in me drove me again to the open. I ran for the rock, feeling that the old man might be glad of my company, as I would be of his.

Within a hundred yards of the rock I stopped and stood as if rooted, forgetting myself at the sight of him. Through the gaps of spilling cloud-water I saw him standing on the rock, bareheaded, his long white hair lying like loose rope ends about his head. He was talking. His voice reached me indistinctly, sounding like an intonation. He was addressing someone or something that lay hidden by the ridge of drooping violets.

A thought flashed through my mind with the speed of the forked lightning that sizzled overhead. It was gold he had there; gold, glittering in the soft rain-water, and old Midas was worshipping before his shrine!

As I stood there watching the drenched, crabbed figure, I was seized with hot resentment and disgust. To dare, there in the open, under the eye of the angry gods of the elements, obtrude his paltry greed!

"Shame! Shame on you! Shame!" I cried again and again. Then I ran to the barn to get away from him, thankful in my heart that gold had never meant that much to me.

When the sun came out I wrung out my clothes and hung them out to dry; then in clean things I went out into the clean world and found ripe mulberries to feast on. After that I strolled off to the sandstone bluffs and wandered in and out of caves where once aborigines had made their home.

The sun had set, and the shadowed noise of creeping things sent me barnward. I did not go out after my supper that night, nor did the old man come after me to offer it. I rolled into my saddle blanket and went to sleep, hoping that my impressions of him were wrong, and resolved to get away, anyway, in two or three days more.

The old man awoke me in the morning. He stood over me, crying excitedly: "Get up! Get up! The dam's broken—the wheel has stopped! We must get to work at it right away!"

The breakwater that forced the current from the centre of the river to the side of the bank where the wheel turned was broken by a freshet from the storm. While I was filling and carrying sacks of sand to mend the break, the old man was busy working at the wheel, nailing loose boards on it, and tightening nuts here and there.

I paid little attention to him, nor did I know that my work on the breakwater was slowly driving the current under the wheel, where it might start to turn at any time.

That was just what did happen. The water-wheel was started going by the force of the current under it. The old man, who was hanging on top of it wrenching at a bolt, fell ten or twelve feet down into shallow water.

The noise of the splash hurried me to him. As I pulled him out, blood was oozing from the side of his head. I thought that he was killed, and I was alarmed and sorry. Taking him in my arms—and he was heavy enough—I struggled to the top of the bank.

Gently I laid him down and felt his pulse. It was pitiably weak. His blood wet the grass. I tore off my shirt and bound up his head. The sun was over the mountain-top sending down waves of heat. There was no shade this side of the violet rock or barn, and ugly flies were buzzing about. It was a long way to the rock, but, I thought, suppose it was. The chance was that he was dying, and, after all, why shouldn't he be near the thing that he prized most in life, whatever it might be? I placed my arms around his hips and slung his trunk to my shoulder. In this way I carried him to the fence, found the gate, and squeezed him through. Then easing him from my shoulder, I laid him down on the green, alongside the rock.

He groaned aloud and made an effort as if to rise. Surely, I thought, he must have some kind of medicine around here that will restore him to consciousness. Timidly, I don't know why, I started to explore the rock. When I came to the river end of it, I found a door.

There, right before the door, was one of the largest rattlesnakes I have ever seen. Coiled he was, and ready for a fight. In an instant I forgot everything but that snake. I grabbed a piece of mahogany firewood and killed him on the spot.

The door was fastened with a padlock, the frames set loosely in the lava rock. I jumped at it with

OLD MAN OF THE VIOLET ROCK

both feet, being by this time so excited that I hardly knew what I was doing. The door flew off its frail hinges and daylight stopped short, at a curtain of inner gloom.

It was a cave, and dark. A hibernating odour percolated out of it. Ugh! What a place to live in, I thought, for now I had no doubt that this was the old man's home. I took a step or two forward, then hesitated. Suppose there were snakes here, too? My flesh crept and I retreated, only to be prompted to effort of some kind by a groan from outside.

My eyes becoming accustomed to the darkness, I could now see a feeble ray of light, proceeding, it seemed, from a hole in the roof. I went slowly and carefully ahead. Gradually things began to take form: the old man's bed, shoes underneath, a chair, a box or two. No table as yet, no stove. But these, I thought, would reveal themselves when I should reach the shaft of light.

I kept moving on, conscious of a warning to beware. The hair on my head straightened, I was as springy on my feet as a wild cat, and my heart gave pile-driving blows. Then I reached a sort of inner room where the light fell, and my muscles set like the click of a bear-trap.

There, sitting on a chair by a table, was a skeleton! Evidently it had been a woman, and before it, on the table, was a great bunch of violets, still starry with morning dew. As my muscles gradually relaxed I tiptoed closer.

It was plain that years had passed since her life went out. Much of the long black hair that had been hers, remained. Time had not parched that, and in the sunken, dried-up eyes, the parchment cheeks, the slender neck, the puckered, pointed mouth, was evidence that once she may have been beautiful.

One side of her face had been artfully turned to conceal the bones where the light, leathery skin had fallen off. But the breast and ribs stood out starkly, and on the arms and hands skin still clung only in little patches. Around the waist was tucked a khaki shirt, and the legs and feet were, from where I stood, invisible.

I was overcome by a sort of reverence. The violets on the table sent forth the essence of beauty, and I knew that I was standing within a shrine—a shrine sacred to Love and Beauty. My mind became permeated with the picture of the past as though it had not perished. . . . Young and beautiful she had been, and full of life, dwelling with her lover in the sandstone cave above the river, grinding the nuts he brought her for food, and decking out her hair for him with desert flowers. Then something happened that killed the pleasure of the vision. The present flipped back ruthlessly, and I was overcome with sorrow for having intruded on the old man's love. I must hasten at once to retrace my steps and help him.

There was a sound behind me, somewhat louder than a baby makes when it breathes the sting of life into its delicate body. It was a cry that would have meant nothing to an unknowing listener, but it voiced for the one that uttered it, life, death, passion, and despair.

Through the darkness came the old man, staggering towards me. "You thought I was dead, did you?" His voice seemed to fill the cave. "You've killed the snake that guarded me for years. And now you have found Her. Go away and leave me. All I ask is that you do not tell. There is money under my pillow. Take what you think you have earned. But go! Go! Leave me! I must be alone!"

He knelt down by the skeleton as he spoke, and great tears ran down unhindered over the crusted blood on his hand. Without a word I turned and walked out of the cave. Money I did not want from that old man. My misty eyes sought the sunshine.

I made for the barn, saddled my horse, and rode up the river, silently, solemnly, past the violets and the lone rock, past the old water-wheel. It was groaning again with its laden buckets, and this seemed to me a good omen. I felt that the old man would be all right again. I rode on for some time, and at length drew up at a little farm about twelve miles from the rock.

A Spaniard who lived there, raising a few sheep, told me about the snake; how the old man had pulled out his fangs and made almost a companion of him, and how, when he rang a bell, the snake would come to him. When I heard this I was filled with deep regret, which I shall never cease to feel, for having killed the old man's pet. I learned, too, the old man's name: John Dakin, the Spaniard called him. I realized that this was perhaps the first time that it never had occurred to me to try to find out someone's name. I had been content to think of him merely as the Old Man. The Spaniard said that he had been a cultured, wealthy man, and an archæologist, and of his own accord had settled in these parts. He had become a kind of hermit, of whom no one knew much, except that he cared not to speak to any man. Of his treasured romance, his precious flowers, his living dead, the Spaniard did not know, nor did I enlighten him.

CHAPTER THIRTY-ONE

HORSE PLAY

Two days later I rode into Jordan Valley, Oregon, a cattle and sheep country. I came upon a little town in the heart of the valley, and remained there one day. It was a sorry day for me, as I had to leave town on foot, after gambling my horse away.

I had met an old prospector who had a horse as good as mine, and together we had come on a farmer, driving into town with an old buckboard to sell. It was cheap: twelve dollars he asked for it. As matters stood it was of no use to me, nor to the prospector either, each of us having but one horse. Yet we both wished we could have it, as it was built for two horses and roomy, and a stout hazel-wood neck-yoke stuck out in front.

"Well," said the prospector, as we felt the spokes and examined the tyres, "we both can't have it, but I have a scheme for one of us getting it."

"What's that?" I asked.

"Come over to the hotel," he said, "there's dice there, honest dice. One flop out of the box—aces high. The high dice takes both horses."

For a moment my mind wandered back to San Francisco, to my dice game of tops and bottoms, the last game I had played. I had learned a lot since then, but the thought of the comfortable buckboard, and the obvious honesty of the old prospector, made me take another chance.

"Come on," said I, "it shall be as you say."

"You understand," he said, "the high dice takes both horses."

"How about the saddles?"

"Everything goes with the horse, and one flop out of the box settles it."

He shook first and rolled two fives.

I shook the dice; I blew on them; I swung them over my head three times. When they rolled on to the mahogany bar, two threes were all I had. Sadly I watched the prospector drive away with the two horses hitched to the buckboard.

Then commenced a series of makeshifts for me. I footed it through the hills and desert, getting work wherever I could to earn enough money for a grub-stake, always with the prospector's thought that sooner or later I should strike it rich.

Then one day I discovered a ledge not far from Mono Lake, California. "At last," said I, "at last!"

The ledge had all the earmarks of a mine. It was three feet across, with a perfect wall, dipping at an angle of forty-five degrees. The ore was free milling, and although low grade on the surface it warranted working for depth to find rich values.

I set about with a feeling of optimism that I had never before experienced. For three months I worked and starved. I had to pack my grub sixteen miles, and poor grub it was. Boiled beans for breakfast, cold beans for lunch, and warmed-over beans for supper. Day in and day out I ate the same food. There was no one to speak to, no news, and no new thoughts—work, only work.

Sometimes I would get discouraged. Then I would look at the beautiful sugarloaf quartz in the ledge, and my eye would catch a little glint of gold. That was all I needed to go at it with fresh vigour.

One morning I made up my mind to go away. I was a slave to a rainbow and I knew it, and I wanted to break away for ever. I knew that if ever I did break away I should never return to this or any other mine—unless in later saner years.

Even then it is doubtful if my resolution would have held, had it not been for a farmer. Fate surely brought him that very morning, mounted on one horse, and leading another, with rifles slung across the saddles.

"Have you a little time to spare?" he called, stopping at the mouth of my tunnel.

"Yes," I answered. "All kinds of time."

"Then come along with me," he said. "Get on this horse and take this rifle. Three Mexicans killed the sheriff this morning. We're out after them. Come on."

Before I had time to more than snatch my coat we were off at a gallop down the mountain trail. I was never to see that mine again, and I suppose some other poor prospector got the benefit of my worn outfit; ragged blanket, blunt pick, beans, glittering hopes, and whatever else there was.

For about three miles we rode silently, the farmer well in the lead, and I holding to my horse as best I could, for he was anything but tame. My mind was swirling, wondering about the outcome before sundown.

We reined up in a little meadow where we were joined by four other horsemen, farmers also, one of them cross-eyed and carrying a Springfield rifle. I wondered how he could be of any use on a man-hunt. He was of very little, as was shown before the day was out. His gun *nearly* went off numberless times—so many things he thought he saw—and when it *did* go off it was not his fault that no one was hurt.

"We're on their trail, boys," he shouted. "All we have to do is to keep after them." Then he went on to tell how the bandits had broken into a store and stolen arms, including a Savage rifle, which he had been told could kill a man at a distance of two miles. These murdering Mexicans were supposedly Pancho Villa's soldiers, revolutionists who had crossed the line into California.

We scoured the hills, and about four o'clock came to where they lay behind some fallen timber. They were full of fight, and opened fire on us without warning. The first shot killed the horse on which I was riding, the second took a sliver out of the cross-eyed farmer's chin—which was a pity for the hurt, but undoubtedly a blessing for taking his mind off his gun.

It looked as if we were to be at the mercy of the Mexicans. Everything was in their favour, as we were in the open, without reach of shelter. However, two of our posse were Spanish-American War veterans and good shots, whose presence saved me, at least. As one of the "hombres" raised his head above the fallen timber to shoot again, an ex-soldier silenced him for all time; and so it went with the second and the third, without further casualty to us.

We tied them on to saddles and packed them to the coroner, who received ten dollars from the county for pronouncing them dead. The road house at the head of Mono Lake where the sheriff had been killed, was crowded with country folk waiting for news of the desperadoes. Farmers' wives whose dear ones had joined in the hunt were there, sweethearts of the dead sheriff hung around the corpse tearfully; and the old widow whose house, barn, and stacks of hay the Mexicans had burned was also there bewailing her loss.

Altogether it seemed a fine chance for the prosecuting attorney to square himself with the public, so he ordered drinks for the crowd, and addressed them impressively, telling them everything they already knew, to their great interest. Nevertheless, when the oration was over, and the dead sheriff had been given more homage than he had ever received in life, while the Mexicans were properly reviled, I emerged into the open air thoughtfully.

It was the farmers I was thinking of : the courage of them, going off that morning of their own accord, leaving their wives and children, their stock and growing crops to which they might never return, to perform a dangerous duty—the duty that they felt they owed to society. They were willing to stake their all for the operation of the laws of Justice that they had derived from the usage of the ages.

CHAPTER THIRTY-TWO

ONE WHO SANG

As I walked along that September night thinking of abstract things, I heard away off in the distance the sound of a banjo. It sounded cheerful, after the sad jangle I had just left, and I turned towards it, walking along the lake.

Now the sound became plainer, and I could hear a man's voice, old and cracked, singing a rebel song:

> " When first I joined the army
> My mother said to me,
> 'Come back, you red-headed son of a gun,
> And brand the brindle steer.' "

Words and music came back to me, re-echoed from a small island in the lake, and I followed them to the smudge of a fire, where the old man sat.

Two youngsters were sitting with him and he was entertaining them, more, it seemed, for the love of his song than for the sake of their proffered bottle.

They made me welcome, and the old man continued his song. He had a violin with which he alternated the banjo. Then he would tell stories about all sorts of things, for his had been a queer and roving life. A travelling circus man for years and years, he was able to do a little something anywhere he might be needed.

The young men went off somewhere when they had heard enough, and I was about to start away, being drawn by a cat-like feeling for my own little camp. I turned to say good-bye to the old man.

"Where do you sleep?" I asked.

"Oh," he answered, "I sleep here in the brush. That is, when I can find my blankets."

"Do you always go to bed drunk?" I asked, laughing.

The old fellow began to sob, and I, thinking he was none too sober then, was about to turn away, when he cried:

"No, I don't go to bed drunk. I am almost blind. I'm hard put upon, once the sun sets. When he shines in the sky I'm all right."

Stabbed now by his sobs, I sat down beside him and gave him a sympathetic ear. He told me that he sang, fiddled and played the banjo for the food and the few dimes the people gave him.

"No one will give me work any more. They don't want me. Why should they? I'm of no use in the world. I should die, damn it! Yes, I should die. But"—for his pessimism, never too strong, had run itself out—"I *could* work, I know I could. I'm a tough old geezer yet."

I gathered wood and rekindled the fire, and he and I talked until Mars lit up the dawn sky. It was a strange thing, meeting this old man, and it had far-reaching consequences for me and for others who

ONE WHO SANG

didn't know me any better than the loons who cawed on Mono Lake.

I was moved that night as I had never been moved before, perhaps by the stories of his youth which raised in me memories of my own; perhaps by the aged helplessness of him. I almost thought that some unseen power was bidding me take charge of him, so blind and helpless, and at the mercy of the passer-by.

When daylight came I saw his eyes. Pitiful they were, like those of a blind dog, with sagging under-lids and a lifeless look. But one was a little better than the other, and I felt that for the one there was hope, could I but get him to a doctor.

It was four hundred miles to an eye specialist, eighty to the railroad, and I had nineteen dollars in my pocket. Nevertheless, I made the first move by hiring a horse from a farmer for ten dollars, with the promise to send him back from Bishop.

I launched the old man—Austen was his name, and that seemed to be all the name he had—up on the horse, with a blanket over the animal's bare back. The banjo over his shoulder, the fiddle under one arm, with the other he held on for dear life to the horse's mane.

They laughed at us as we passed the hotel where the sheriff's funeral was about to take place, and we laughed back: Austen because he laughed at himself as much as anyone could laugh at him, and I because the air was sweet and I had something different to do, caring for someone else than myself.

WIDE SEAS AND MANY LANDS.

So we jogged off through the desert, the dust in our throats, the coyotes howling at us. Still the sun shone, and the firelight sparkled, and we laughed.

Four days we marched, stopping for coffee and pork and beans, and the oats which I carried on my back, for the horse. It was a bit hard on the old man going down the steep hills—going up he didn't mind. He was constantly surging forward on to the horse's neck, damning him for not holding his head up.

On the afternoon of the fourth day we came to Bishop, and I scoured the town to raise a subscription to send the old man to Los Angeles. Heartless the people there seemed, and heartless they were. They were not interested in blind men, and urged me to send him to the poor farm, if I could get him in.

I arranged with a cattle man to take the horse back to Mono Lake, and after a night in the town and a real feed, we set out towards Death Valley, where I knew that I could get work to keep us both, and eventually send Austen to Los Angeles.

CHAPTER THIRTY-THREE

OLD AUSTEN SEES DAYLIGHT

WE walked about eight miles that morning. The old fellow was getting tired and we sat down to rest. On the slope of the hill, less than a mile away, stood a modern farm-house, different from any other in the valley. The road approaching it was graded and wide: young trees lined its sides in uniform growth; alfalfa was growing in the fields, where some beautiful Percheron mares were running and playing with their stocky colts. Jersey cows with limbs like fawns were nibbling the grass. An old Indian with a noble bearing stood motionless as a statue; shovel in hand, watching the tiny irrigation ditches, which, if untended, were so tricky with the unset soil of that country.

A white mongrel dog who was out chasing rabbits ran to us, barking and wagging his tail. I patted him, and he licked the old man's hands. Then barking again in a friendly way, he ran into his home road and stood, his head over his shoulder, as if urging us to come.

" That dog is our first friend in five days, Austen,"

I said, "and I'll bet that his master is kind and considerate, too. Let's go up."

We did go, and we found a child of four or five years playing on the lawn, and a woman in her early thirties unharnessing a horse.

"Let me do that," I offered.

"You don't look as if you knew how," said she, with a quick, keen glance, as she threw back her powerful shoulders.

"Where does the harness go?" I asked, taking it from her.

"First door to the right as you go into the barn. Put the horse in the last stall, and the halter hanging on the iron hook," she said. Then, "Frances," she called to the child, "come here and show this man how to feed Slim and water him."

The child came fearlessly, and I, who thought it was a joke, found it was no joke at all. Several work-horses were in the barn finishing their dinner, and the little girl told me all about them, their names and how they were fed.

As the little girl and I came out of the barn hand-in-hand, the mother was standing talking to Austen, and I saw that she was in full possession of the facts of our case. I learned in turn that she was hanging on to this ranch, which she had been forced to mortgage heavily, in the forlorn hope of selling it at a time when war had driven value out of land everywhere. People were keeping their cash, not knowing what would happen, and she felt that if she could not sell she must

OLD AUSTEN SEES DAYLIGHT

leave the place she had redeemed from the desert, and start another trail.

While she fed us—and it seemed as if we could never stop eating the good ranch food that was really fit for workmen—she talked to us, and we consulted about Austen's eyes. She seemed to feel at once that it was as much her responsibility as it was his, or mine.

"I can give him work about the house for a while," she said, "until we can arrange about the doctor in Los Angeles. That part of it I will answer for, if you will take him down there. When he gets through I will let him irrigate for me and pay me back. More than that I cannot promise, for I expect to rent the ranch this winter and move away."

"You are the trouble for me," she continued, "for you are a sailor and an Irishman, and I never hire sailors or Irishmen. Sailors always want their own way, and Irishmen are here one minute, and then get angry and leave the next."

I thought it better to dispute the premise than to argue the conclusion, so I denied that I was either a sailor or an Irishman.

"I didn't suppose you'd admit it," she said, "they never do. But you are both. I know you are a sailor because you walk like one, and always will, and an Irishman because that is written all over you."

In vain I protested, for I saw that she meant what she said. I told her what I could do, and how well I could do it. I promised that the best man she had should never be able to set a pace for me. Finally she consented to give me a trial.

I do believe that for a month I worked as I had never worked before, and I must say that I was driven without mercy. But I was well fed and had a little house to myself, and the child, at least when she was not busy with Austen, who fascinated her completely, was kind to me.

My month was up and it was pay-day. I was called into the house and the little girl told me that her mother was going to Bishop, and wanted me to go with her.

We went in the mountain wagon, the child on my knees, the mother driving. She told me when she started that she was going to buy a few things, because she had arranged for Austen to go down to the hospital the next day, and for me to go and stay with him.

I looked down at my worn boots, for I had been grubbing sage brush and digging ditches.

"Yes, I know," she said kindly, catching the look. "You'll have a chance to get them."

As we started south on the train next day she told me that she had sold a cow to get the ready money to pay and send us!

At the hospital I found plenty to do with the old man. I held his hand while Dr. McCoy operated, stitching up the curtain of film, not a cataract, as he described it, to either eyelid. Then there was the cheering of him through the dismal days that followed.

Five days later the doctor took the poor old man's bandages off, and he nearly went wild with joy. He could see perfectly with one eye and almost as well with the other. He shouted and sang, and kissed all the nurses. He was the circus man of the 'sixties again, and the " Brindle Steer " rang out until it was suppressed by a nervous attendant.

The doctor would not take a cent for the operation. He was one of God's creatures, too.

Austen and I were given a happy greeting when we came back to the ranch. The lady's cow money had brought us back again. All shared in the joy of that old man: joy in beholding the valleys, the green grass, and the mountain streams, to say nothing of the sight of his banjo, with its seasoned strings.

That night, in the sitting-room before the fire, he sang songs of other days, of the musket and the broadsword, and his old-young voice rang with happiness. He wound up a little raggedly with:

" When first I joined the army
My mother said to me———"

As he came to the lines, " ' Come back, you red-headed———' " he broke down and cried as he had that first night, for the very opposite reason.

Austen was given a house to live in and work to do. I did not linger on. I told the lady that

I was going—my mind was made up. Either she should marry me at Christmas in Los Angeles, where I was going to look for work, or I should never see her again.

I went to Los Angeles, getting in touch with what seemed to be an excellent mining proposition, a new town. At Thanksgiving I returned to the ranch for a few days and found that she had written to her father and received his reply. I was a fortune-hunter and an impossible person.

So did my impulsive sacrifice for Austen cause the utmost disturbance thousands of miles away. How was I, who had always worked hard and never valued money, to prove that the prospects of this lonely lady and her people were of no interest to me? Or that, although I had no money, I had some valuable assets of experience, and honesty, and heart?

Then a member of the family appeared, confronting me with a written questionnaire. Said I:

" Indeed, I'll not answer those questions. If you want to look me up, here are the addresses of my enemies. Go to them, for my friends won't interest you."

Surely enough he did, and heard the worst of me, and much that wasn't true, besides. And my lady must needs pay her price, too, for the rescue of a blind man and the sale of a cow——

Her family came to know that I cared nothing for the glitter of all their gold.

OLD AUSTEN SEES DAYLIGHT

If Gold makes for Happiness,
Then Ebb Tide float me out beyond the bar;
Ring your market bells!
Sell your slaughter!
Better the drift weed with its glint of Love,
From a lone star.

CHAPTER THIRTY-FOUR

IRELAND AGAIN

It was the summer of 1925, and I was going to sea again. Not as a sailor before the mast this time, nor as a mate, nor as master, but merely a passenger. I was bound for my old home in Ireland. After thirty years I was going back to the old Dart! As I crowded aboard the steamship, I had as timid a feeling as if I had milched the school and was anticipating a dressing down. Yet there wasn't anyone in Ireland living now, I supposed, to take me to task for my waywardness. With the thought came one of sadness. What would I find there? Memories? Remembrances? Little else, I feared.

As the ship nosed her way towards Ambrose Channel, and the land faded away into the blue of sea and sky, another feeling of lonesomeness came over me. This was not the Atlantic as I knew it. I missed the barefoot sailors, and the smell of hemp and tar, and the blue-nosed mate with the double jaw, yelling, " Lay aloft there, damn youse, and overhaul them topsail buntings ! " No, no clank from blocks, nor flop of sails; instead the steady purr of the ship's engines, and speed away ! " In seven days we'll be in Liverpool," the first officer

IRELAND AGAIN

told me. I recollected the time I crossed this ocean last. Thirty-six days it took, and hellish days they were, every one of them.

As the ship wore away to the east'ard, and the passengers quieted down, blanketed in their chairs, I rambled the decks like a tourist experiencing a first sea voyage. This ocean palace was strange to me. All that reminded me of the old days were the ship's bells. Their tone was the same, and faithfully to their age-long responsibility they chimed the pure time of the sun.

One night after the passengers had all gone to their bunks, I crawled forward, up into the eyes of the ship. There I was alone; everything mortal was behind me. A gentle breeze blew across the bows, and I was hardly conscious of being aboard a steamer. As I stood there holding the jack-pole, gazing out into the luminous night, ships, misty yet not dim—sailing ships of every sort, with every sort of canvas, sailed up from the lee.

They bore memory's sails, bellied out to the wind. I knew them all: one after the other, their hulls black or white, their rigs, their painted ports—of course I knew them. Their scars, too, and all the queer things about them. I called them each by name. How fiery the water looked as it dashed over their bows! How gracefully they rode, with the lee rail low! Ships, real ships, the ships of other years!

I was startled by hearing a voice behind me.

"What the hell are you doing up here? This ain't the place for passengers!"

One by one my ships sank into the jewelled night waters, perhaps to float again when the spirit of memory walks unhindered.

Two days later the ship arrived in Liverpool, and that night I took the Channel boat for Ireland. In the morning I arrived in Belfast, and that afternoon I rode into the little village where I was born.

"Well, well, well!" said the farmers, gathered round, selling their cartloads of potatoes. "So ye're back again. And ye don't remember wan of us, that ye don't." They closed around me.

"He looks like his father, God rest his soul," said one.

"G'wan. It's his mother's side of the family he takes after," said another.

Then a little old man walked up to the group. "It's not forgetting me ye'll be, me boy? And it's forty years ago since ye carved yere name on me barn door. Sure, and it's there yet, that it is!"

Another spoke. "It's fooling us he is. Ye mind the time when ye were a wee boy and ye used to scare the very divil out of us with yere ghost stories?"

I laughed to think of the reputation that was mine without my knowing it.

They pointed to a grey wrinkled man coming along. "See him! That's John Rooney. Ye mind him, ye do? The time ye stuck yere cap under the tail of the mare he was riding? Look at the shoulder of him hanging low to this day!"

IRELAND AGAIN

"Yes, I remember that," I said, "and the terrible whipping I got, too."

One by one they plied me with questions. A man with a beard of fall-leaf colouring remarked, "You mind the big tree that we killed the wild cat in?" Of course I did. I loved to climb its broad limbs. "Well, you wouldn't know that tree to-day. I have a wireless coming out of it, me boy." The big sunburned face of him lit up with pride.

Another man left his cart of spuds and walked over holding out his hand.

"It's not saying ye are that ye don't know me? My name is Fitzsimmons. Don't ye remember, we played in the band together?"

"Oh, yes," said I, "you have the farm at Ballywooden."

"That's me—the same man—still living."

"Joe," I said, "some years ago I dreamed about your farm."

"Ye did now? Well, let's hear it." Then turning to a couple who were talking among themselves: "Keep yere tongue in yere teeth. Not a word out of yez till we hear what he has to say."

"Well, Joe," I went on, "you know the little field by the big river? There's a patch there, as I remember it, that never grew anything."

"Go on," urged Fitzsimmons with intense interest.

"Well, I dreamed that in that part of the field there lay a mine."

"Be heavens, isn't that wonderful now! Let me tell ye something," he said excitedly, tapping me on the shoulder. "Two years ago an expert told me, says he, on that very same spot ye have a deposit of iron ore."

"Is that so now? How near does it come to me?" asked Dick Hanna.

"Right up to your fence," I laughed.

"Go on now, and don't be fooling us all again!"

That evening I stole away, seeking the places I loved as a boy. The colouring had not changed; the hawthorn was there with its fragrant blossoms, and the green fields flounced with golden buck thrilled me. But I missed the thatched cottages. There were none to be seen: cosy brick houses with slate roofs had replaced them. Perhaps they are more comfortable—I suppose so—but I didn't like the looks of them. On I walked past the old haunted castle of Kilklief, till I came to the house where I had my first peep at the world. Strangers were living in it now. My eye roamed away to the hill where the church stood, in the midst of many graves. My folks were all asleep up there now. The wave of sentiment that had been rolling in all day swept over me. I was a boy again. I faced the ocean; unchangeable that. There lay the rock on which the seal used to crawl up and bask himself in the sunny afternoons. I remembered how I used to play my flute for that seal and how he'd nod his head as if he liked my tune. Over there was the old white lighthouse, where the bar still sang its surging song. Farther away the shadows of the night were staggering in from the sea. Below me lay a strip of water, where at an early age I would watch the fairies play. I wondered if those early images might come back. Letting myself down to the strip of water, I straddled a rock and waited. With the gurgle of the sea beneath, and the far-off sound of lowing cattle behind me, I fell into a dreamy state. Nightfall gradually spattered the grey of the day away. There was an unconscious knocking within me at the doors of imagination, as I kept squinting to get a look at my fairies again. Then the conscious mind would rear itself. " Get up, you damned fool! Surely you don't believe in fairies at your time of life? " Still I sat, surrendering myself to the dreams of childhood. What's that behind me, with a moaning drone to it? Surely not the Banshee! I had forgotten all about her. Then I remembered it was a sure sign of death, when she went moaning about. In front of me, I could see the stars dancing as they bathed in the water, and there—yes—three heads. Yes, there they were —the fairies, with their wee red caps, sure enough. Soon they'd come wading towards me and bid me welcome. Carried away by some impulse, I know not what, I rose to my feet to shout a greeting. Then it was that three ducks or more flew out of that strip of water and away to a safer place. For a moment I felt ashamed of myself for sitting there like a loon so long, trying to get another glimpse into that which was for Youth and Youth alone to see.

WIDE SEAS AND MANY LANDS.

The moon, like a disk of hammered gold, floated out of the sea, and the yellow glimmer of it made a primrose trail across the lough. I walked up to the county road, lit a cigarette, and looked at my watch. A quarter to twelve. Heavens, no wonder I was stiff, from sitting so long! I strolled on till I came to the Four Roads. The one ahead went straight on to Strangford. The one to the left was a roundabout way, but this one had memories, and I took it.

As I walked on my thoughts went bounding back to the time when I dared not be out alone this time of night. Why, here was the place the Headless Man was seen! The story had it, that in the flesh he fell in a brawl, and had that part of him kicked off. Once Pat Burke had seen the apparition. He was scared so bad, and he ran so fast, that his heart, poor man, was never the same after it! Yes, and here's another bit of road that has a tale, too. One o'clock in the morning it was, many years ago, a hearse was seen here, drawn by four black horses. And, mind you, devil a bit of noise it made over the cobble-stones, on its way to the graveyard. In the morning when the gossips told about the hearse they shook their heads. "Ah, wurra, wurra, somebody's going to die!" they said. And sure enough, two days later, old Rorry Rice passed out.

As I journeyed on, recalling those tales, I came to a high hawthorn bush. Here was the place where Andy McCann tried a bottle of holy water on an evil spirit. Ah, that was a troublesome

IRELAND AGAIN

spirit, when I was a boy! It would shunt you into a shuch as you passed it by. I heard it said that the reason for its waywardness was that in the flesh it never went to confession. Andy McCann was coming by late one night. Forewarned is forearmed. He had put a bottle of holy water in his pocket. The ghost as usual stepped out in the middle of the road. It took a minute or two for Andy to collect himself. The power to destroy that bad spirit lay in Andy's pocket. He uncorked the bottle and sprinkled a circle in the dusty road. Says he to the ghost: "If ye aren't of the divil step into me circle, and it's a word I'll be having with ye!" The ghost disappeared and Andy walked home, with the bottle gripped tight in his fist.

I stopped when I reached the graveyard. There were so many in there that I had known. Irish Anne, she that could curve a cobble-stone, slept there now. For a moment I was filled with reverence. Should I go in and offer a pagan prayer to the moon, for the privilege of such a night with myself? Then a creepy feeling took possession of me. Shadows from the whin-bushes wagged across the road in front of me. Away off somewhere a dog howled, and howled again. I felt urged to run, as I had forty years ago, but the training of conscious thought and worldly experience had me in leash now. I commenced to reason with myself. True, I was not afraid. But hadn't I lost a pleasure just the same? This conscious balanced thought,

WIDE SEAS AND MANY LANDS.

where did it lead to? A world of the five senses, in which there was no room for imagination or speculation. My wanderings had taken me over wide seas and many lands, but I had to return to the land of my childhood to get the soundings of my North-west Passage.

What's that I hear in the old haunted castle? Whist!

Ach, it's music it is, from the fairy bagpipes